TRAINS OF NEWFOUNDLAND

NF210 941 in Terra Transport paint scheme at Grand Falls, December 27, 1987 (Author photo)

TRAINS OF NEWFOUNDLAND

KENNETH G. PIEROWAY

WITH A FOREWORD BY ROBERT J. SANDUSKY

FLANKER PRESS LIMITED

ST. JOHN'S

Library and Archives Canada Cataloguing in Publication

Title: Trains of Newfoundland / Kenneth G. Pieroway ; with a foreword by Robert J. Sandusky.
Names: Pieroway, Kenneth G., author. | Sandusky, Robert J., writer of foreword.
Description: Includes bibliographical references.
Identifiers: Canadiana (print) 20220398844 | Canadiana (ebook) 20220398941 | ISBN 9781774570920
  (hardcover) | ISBN 9781774570937 (softcover) | ISBN 9781774570944 (PDF)
Subjects: LCSH: Railroad trains—Newfoundland and Labrador—History—20th century—Pictorial works. |
  LCSH: Narrow gauge railroads—Newfoundland and Labrador—History—20th century—Pictorial works.
Classification: LCC TF27.N42 P54 2022 | DDC 625.26022/2—dc23

PRINTED IN CANADA

This paper has been certified to meet the environmental and social standards of the Forest Stewardship Council® (FSC®) and comes from responsibly managed forests, and verified recycled sources.

Cover Design by Graham Blair

FLANKER PRESS LTD.
1243 KENMOUNT ROAD, UNIT 1
PARADISE, NL
CANADA

TELEPHONE: (709) 739-4477   FAX: (709) 739-4420   TOLL-FREE: 1-866-739-4420
WWW.FLANKERPRESS.COM

9 8 7 6 5 4 3 2 1

 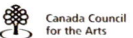 

We acknowledge the [financial] support of the Government of Canada. *Nous reconnaissons l'appui [financier] du gouvernement du Canada.* We acknowledge the support of the Canada Council for the Arts, which last year invested $153 million to bring the arts to Canadians throughout the country. *Nous remercions le Conseil des arts du Canada de son soutien. L'an dernier, le Conseil a investi 153 millions de dollars pour mettre de l'art dans la vie des Canadiennes et des Canadiens de tout le pays.* We acknowledge the financial support of the Government of Newfoundland and Labrador, Department of Tourism, Culture and Recreation for our publishing activities.

Dedicated to the memory of my dad, World War II RCAF veteran George Israel Pieroway (1923–1967). The sacrifices that you and your comrades made gave us the freedom we enjoy today. Lest we forget. Thank you for adopting me and introducing me to our Newfoundland narrow-gauge trains as a young boy. By doing both, you gave me the gift of life and a lifetime of passion.

Westbound freight at Harry's Brook, June 19, 1956 (Robert J. Sandusky photo)

CONTENTS

These are our Super Beagle sketches.

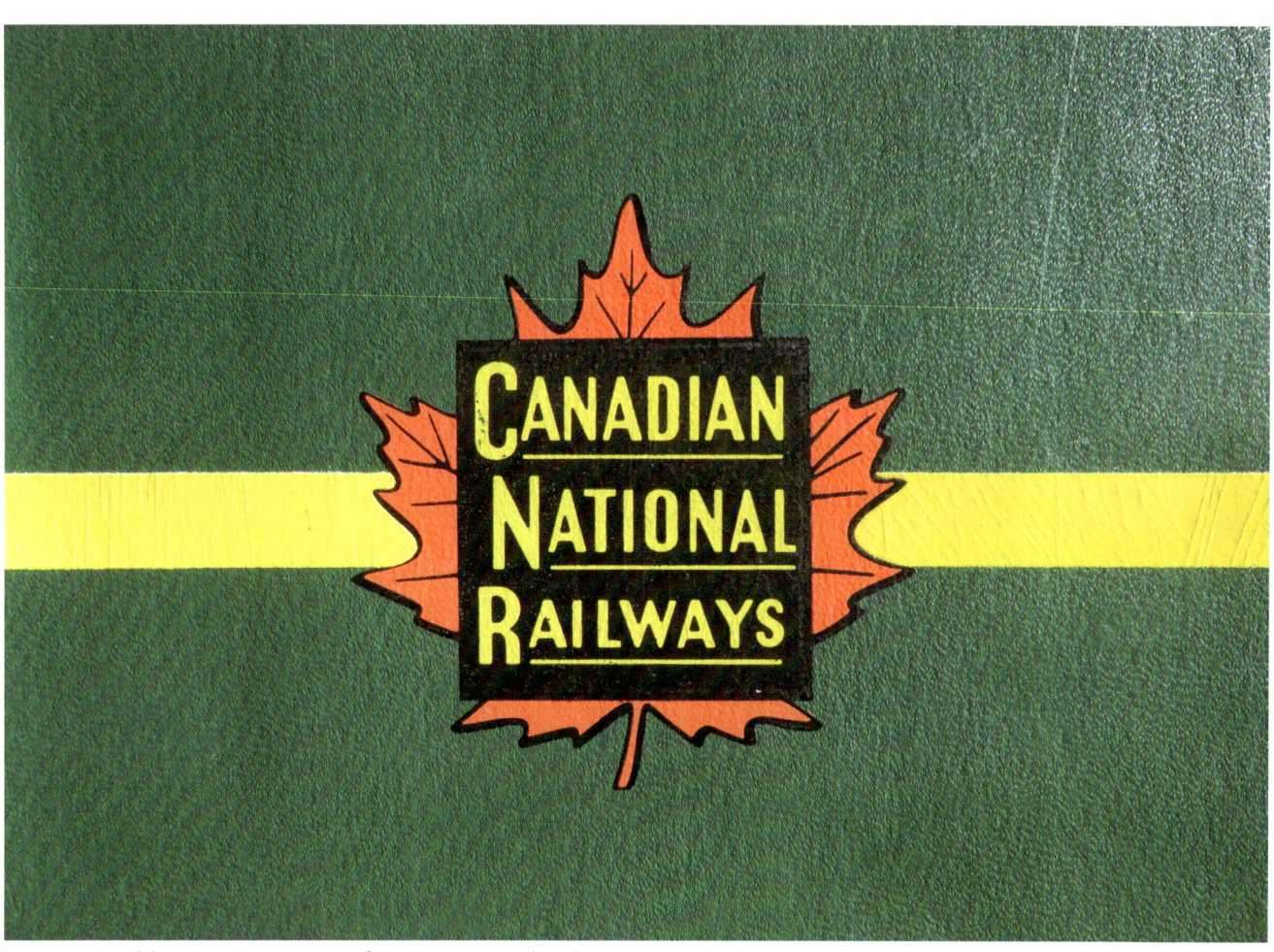

1954 timetable cover (Courtesy of Wayne Greenland)

FOREWORD

PHOTOGRAPHING THE ROCK

This writer began life with scant knowledge of "The Rock" save for adventurous bits passed on from a co-worker who had originated there. Perhaps some scarce selections in a geographic journal? As well, several acquaintances in the rail transportation business had been there and showed selected evidence of the railway operations there. I found it quite interesting and hoped to visit it sometime.

Newfoundland's arrival into Canadian confederation brought along its major railway system as well. This meant likely governance under the Canadian National Railways. The unpredictable outcome of this fact galvanized a small group of this writer's historic- and railway-minded friends into planning a short visit, in June 1956, to Newfoundland. It included both government and private railway operations there. Most railway operations in Newfoundland were then still steam-powered, which was something to be recorded for posterity.

Time moved quickly, and even as our visiting group had completed our railway tour, there were new diesel locomotives arriving in St. John's and immediately entering service. Whilst appreciating the retirement of this "era of steam," we did not yet guess that all the railway operations in Newfoundland would be gone by the end of 1988.

In the intervening years, this writer (captured by the magnetic effect of the island) managed three more visits. Included was one during the last week of passenger service in 1969, and again in 1975, which meant three more opportunities to explore and photograph a combination of railway and scenic subjects.

My final opportunity was in 1984, with my wife, three children, and a camper. We put in beside a roadside hill on the Trans-Canada Highway between Rantem and Tickle Harbour. We had been trailing a long, eastbound freight, and this rocky hill was an exciting (for family) outlook for a picnic as well as a good viewpoint for the eventually arriving freight train (exciting for Dad).

With train passed and lunch done, we then spent some Newfoundland time sorting out the differences among Labrador tea, crackerberry, partridgeberry, and bakeapple plants. Our destination had been St. John's to see the Queen's Royal Yacht and Her Majesty Queen Elizabeth II. However, her visit got cancelled because of a newly called federal election (and we did get a glance at her yacht)!

In later years, I had the good fortune to meet Ken Pieroway and acquaint him with my collection of Newfoundland railway scenes accumulated over a period of 28 years. It is gratifying to know that they have been useful for him in illustrating the views of the beautiful island and the railway that it served.

Time moves on relentlessly, as does the diminishing number of those who carry and treasure the memories of the Newfoundland Railway and its famous *Caribou*, be they former employee, passenger, historian, or just an observer passing from afar.

Trains of Newfoundland may be interpreted as a celebration of the railway in the form of an end-to-end farewell "voyage" as the reader "boards" in St. John's and travels the length of the railway mainline to Port aux Basques. The place names, some familiar (and possibly some forgotten), will move by as do the seasons. Perhaps a familiar face will be seen. Who knows?

It is hoped that you have a pleasant journey!

Robert J. Sandusky
Oakville, ON
March 31, 2022

Harry's Brook, June 19, 1956 (Robert J. Sandusky photo)

Preface

I've always loved trains. In fact, I can't remember not ever loving them. From the moment my dad took me down to the station in Corner Brook as a toddler in the mid-1960s and I saw my first CNR green and gold diesel. With its engine roaring and exhaust stacks spewing and two blasts from the horn, I was hooked for life. That was the start of a passion that is just as strong, if not even stronger, almost 60 years later. Since 1987, I've ridden over Newfoundland's Gaff Topsails five times, crossed Canada twice on VIA Rail, and have had many dozens of other rail journeys in the US, the UK, and throughout continental Europe with my wife, Michelle, by my side. Hopefully, there will be many more to come.

The 704-mile Newfoundland Railway was the longest narrow-gauge system on the entire continent of North America. It's been close to 35 years since the last trains ran in Newfoundland, and much has been written to commemorate the occasion, including two coffee table books by me. *Rails Across the Rock*, released in 2013, was a then-and-now look at the mainline, while *Rails Around the Rock*, released a year later, explored the branch and industrial lines in the same format. Numerous other authors, such as Bill Baggs, Clayton Cook, Bren Dicks, Mont Lingard, Bill Linley, and Robert Hunt also celebrated in print and photographs what the Newfoundland Railway was to our Island. It's been covered in articles and editorials in various newspapers, magazines, and commemorative television stories, and many other national railway books have chapters featuring it as well. Several websites on the Internet are now devoted to it, where rail fans post pictures and stories of that bygone time.

For me, the story is not yet fully told and may in fact never be. That is my impetus for this book. I have amassed such a great collection of colour images with heartwarming generosity from North America's finest railway photographers, from Robert J. Sandusky to Stan J. Smaill, from James A. Brown to Steve Bradley, from Robert Palmer to Steve Patterson. The list goes on, and these images are so breathtakingly beautiful that they have to be seen and shared while the opportunity still presents. I am keenly aware that many collections over the years have been lost forever, never to see the light of day again to be appreciated by the legions of rail fans and others.

This book was originally intended to be another "then-and-now," but upon several scouting trips to locate the exact spots where once the photographers stood, I began to realize that, with nature reclaiming what was once hers, the overgrowth of trees and vegetation obscured many reference points. With that, more than half of my photos would be rendered useless for comparison, and it would be a real tragedy not to include them. Following discussions with my publisher, it was agreed by all that these images were too important to be excluded, and a decision to go with an all-original record was decided upon.

Like my earlier efforts, this one started with a single image. This time from Richard Manicom of a 1964 *Caribou* passenger train dressed in the CNR green and gold about to depart St. John's for Port aux Basques. It was the same type of train I remembered from my childhood and—who knows?—perhaps one of those I saw with my dad when it arrived in Corner Brook later the next day. With that, the seed was planted for another cross-island journey, and before long, I had many beautiful images from my old photographer friends, such as Bill Linley and Rich Taylor, and my new ones, such as John Freyseng. The pebble of train-watching that my dad threw into the pond of life so many years ago resulted in ripples that travelled far enough into the future to write this book.

So, sit back and enjoy a wonderful, all-colour train ride from St. John's to Port aux Basques with virtually every stop in between spanning the last four decades of operations. Ride both the steam- and diesel-hauled *Caribou* passenger trains, multiple diesel unit freight trains, little mixed trains on the way to the branch lines, and lengthy mixed trains over the Gaff Topsails. Follow them seaside and through the interior to the little towns that sprang up along the line and marvel at the rugged beauty of this colourful and pristine island. To quote Tom Hanks as the conductor in *The Polar Express* movie, "One thing about trains . . . it doesn't matter where they are going. What matters is deciding to get on."

Author in cupola of caboose 6071 at Gaff Topsail, April 16, 1988 (Paul Moore photo)

Author and wife, Michelle, on VIA's Canadian near Capreol, January 28, 2018 (Peter J. Rickershauser photo)

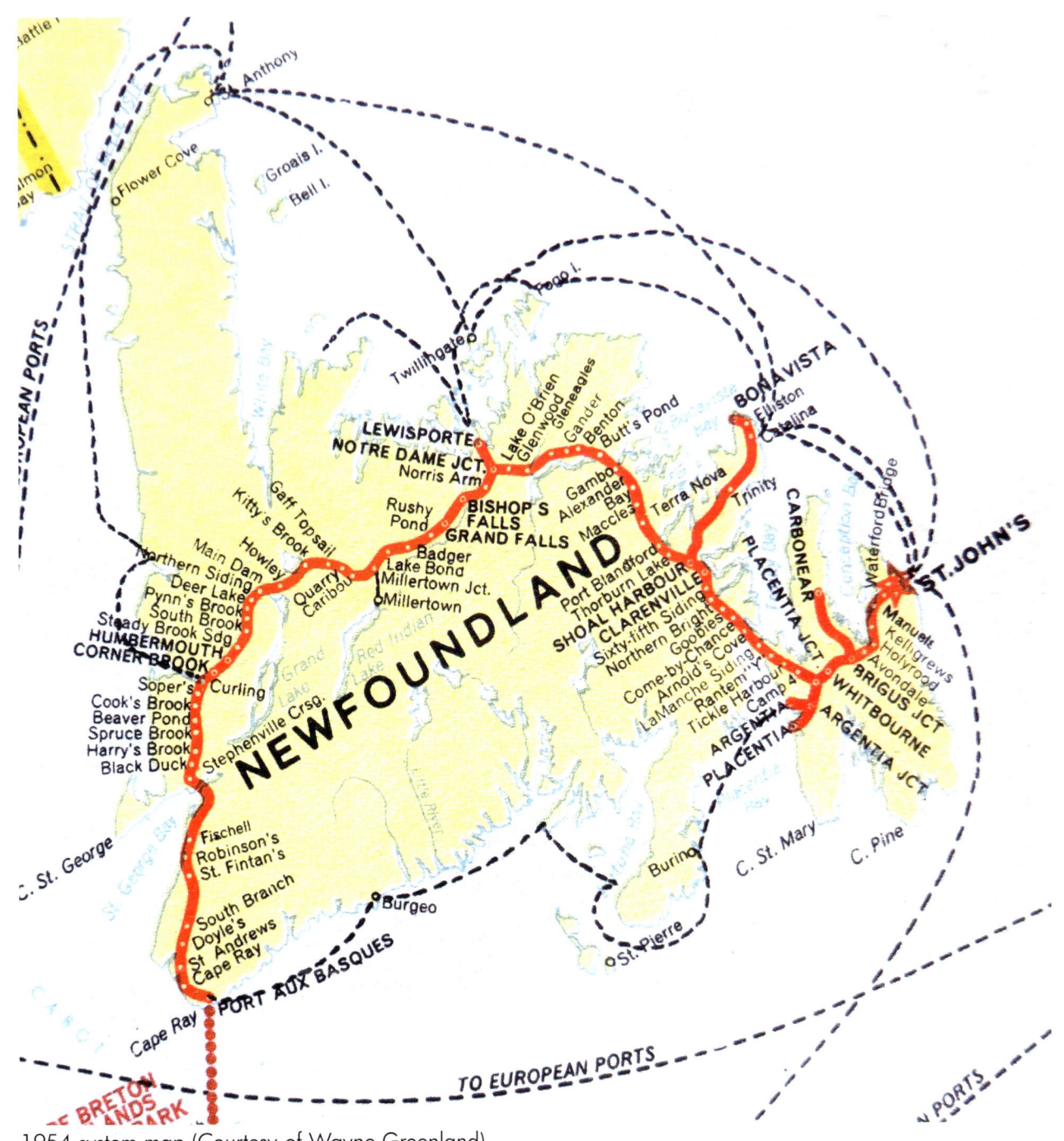

1954 system map (Courtesy of Wayne Greenland)

NR passenger car logo (Author photo)

CONDENSED TIMELINE OF THE NEWFOUNDLAND RAILWAY

June 1, 1881	Incorporation of the Newfoundland Railway Company.
August 16, 1881	Construction commenced at Fort William, St. John's.
January 16, 1882	First experimental train ride to Donovans.
June 1882	First passenger service St. John's to Topsail return.
August 1882	Daily excursion service to Holyrood return.
November 1884	Southern Division, Harbour Grace Railway, St. John's to Harbour Grace completed.
October 2, 1888	Northern Division, Placentia Railway, Whitbourne to Placentia completed.
1893	Halls Bay Railway completed from Placentia Junction to Norris Arm.
1897	Newfoundland Northern and Western Railway completed from Norris Arm to Port aux Basques. Operations taken over by Reid-Newfoundland Company (RNCo.).
1898	Lewisporte Branch completed.
June 30, 1898	First through passenger train from St. John's arrives in Port aux Basques.
June 1, 1903	Trains start running from the new Victorian Station and headquarters on Water Street.
November 8, 1911	Bonavista Branch opened.
January 1, 1914	Trepassey Branch opened.
July 1915	Heart's Content and Bay de Verde Branches opened.
1920	First of ten 4-6-2 Pacific Class locomotives arrive.
July 1, 1923	Government takes over from RNCo., renamed Newfoundland Government Railway.
June 9, 1926	Name restored to Newfoundland Railway. New rolling stock ordered, including Pullman sleepers *Ferryland* and *Harbour Grace*.
1928	First all-steel passenger cars arrive, sleepers *Grand Falls* and *Humber*.
1930	First of thirty 2-8-2 Mikado-class steam locomotives arrive.
1934	Trepassey, Bay de Verde, and Grates Cove Branches abandoned.
1939	Heart's Content abandoned.
1943	Twenty-five new passenger cars acquired from Canadian Car and Foundry (CC&F) under the 1941 lend-lease agreement, including sleepers *Botwood*, *Buchans*, *Gander*, and *Fogo*.
August 1948	The Newfoundland Railway orders three GE 380-HP centre-cab diesel switchers for yard service.
March 31, 1949	Canadian National Railways assumes operation of Newfoundland Railway.
June 1950	CNR renames the trans-island passenger train from *Overland Limited* to *Caribou*.

1952	Six new sleepers acquired: *Clarenville, Flower's Cove, Corner Brook, Princeton, Bishop's Falls,* and *Whitbourne.*
January 1953	First of nine NF110 1,200-HP diesels arrives.
1955	Five new coaches and sleeper *Bonavista* acquired.
August 1956	Six G8 875-HP diesels arrive for branch line service.
November 1956	First of thirty-eight NF210 1,200-HP diesels arrive.
December 1956	Seven steam generator units (SGU) arrive to replace steam locomotives with diesels on the *Caribou.*
March 27, 1957	Last revenue steam locomotive run. Railway mainline fully dieselized.
April 28, 1957	Trains 15 and 16, the tri-weekly Corner Brook–St. John's Express, cancelled and replaced by daily *Caribou* service.
October 5, 1958	Railway post office (RPO) cars reassigned from the *Caribou* to the new trans-island mail and express on Mixed No. 3 and Mixed No. 4.
1958	Final passenger car delivered. Diner 176 the last built for the CNR in Canada.
1961	First batch of five out of twenty steel cabooses built to replace older wooden versions arrives.
May 1967	CN announces plan to replace the *Caribou* with a trans-island bus service.
July 4, 1968	Canadian Transport Commission (CTC) gives CN authority to discontinue the *Caribou.*
October 1, 1968	Railway post office (RPO) service ends on Trains 203 and 204.
November 26, 1968	RoadCruiser bus service begins early. Passengers given option of choosing either bus or train. Bus is favoured 5-1.
July 2, 1969	Train 102, the *Caribou,* departs Port aux Basques for the final time at 10:00 a.m., arrives in St. John's July 3 at 8:00 a.m.
1970	Standard-gauge boxcar to narrow-gauge boxcar truck transfer in full operation in Port aux Basques.
1971	Daily timetable freights 400 and 401 cancelled, leaving only 203 and 204.
March 28, 1977	The Commission of Inquiry into Newfoundland Transportation (a.k.a. the Sullivan Commission) set up.
February 1979	The Sullivan Commission recommends the railway be phased out in ten years.
March 30, 1979	Newfoundland Transportation Division set up for local management of operations.
October 16, 1979	Newfoundland Transportation Division renamed Terra Transport.
October 1980	Terra Transport commences containerization program of replacing boxcars with twenty- and forty-foot intermodal shipping containers.
November 23, 1983	Final run of the *Bonavista* Mixed Train, Terra Transport Mixed Train 205.
May 20, 1984	Final run of the annual Victoria Day *Trouter's Special.*
July 3, 1984	System-wide implementation of the Manual Block System (MBS).
September 19, 1984	Final run of the *Argentia* Mixed Train. Mixed Extra 800 East.
September 20, 1984	Final run of the *Carbonear* Mixed Train. Mixed Extra 804 East.
July 1987	Boxcar service discontinued.
May 4, 1988	Last plow train from Badger to Corner Brook.
June 20, 1988	Roads for Rails Agreement announced to terminate the railway in exchange for $800.6 million for highway improvements.
September 30, 1988	Official shutdown. Mixed Extra 917 West ends all scheduled train service.
October 12, 1988	Rail Removal Program commences. First rail lifted at Mileage 340.
November 16, 1990	Last rail removed at Cannings Lane, Bishop's Falls. The Newfoundland Railway is no more.

Eastbound freight in Stephenville Crossing, June 19, 1956 (Robert J. Sandusky photo)

CN Train 102, eastbound *Caribou* at Bear Cove, June 20, 1967 (John Freyseng photo)

"Up mountains, down valleys, through spruce bush and fir. Over barrens and bleak, where trees grip rocks and grow crippled by the winds, where salt water splashes and subways don't go. Where the caribou roam and moose huddle in yards, where the hunter snares his rabbit and jigs for fat cod. Where small boats chug to sea with gillnets and twine and muscle and heart. Where herring fills the hold and anxious women wait. Where the hawks hover and the gulls soar and partridge feed on the flats. Where beaches stretch and salmon run and water streams pure from up high. Through all this the Bullet goes."

— James Quig, *Weekend Magazine*, February 1, 1969

Train 207 in Holyrood, July 30, 1979 (Tom Nelligan photo)

CHAPTER 1

ST. JOHN'S SUBDIVISION

NEWFOUNDLAND TRANSPORTATION DIVISION

EMPLOYEES' OPERATING TIME TABLE

27

TAKING EFFECT SUNDAY, JUNE 17th, 1979

REFER TO PAGE 1 FOR EFFECTIVE TIME, AND FOR
OTHER TIME AND DATE CHANGES THAT WILL OCCUR.

TEAMWORK PREVENTS ACCIDENTS

R.G. MESSENGER
PRESIDENT AND GENERAL MANAGER
ST. JOHN'S

J.A. TAIT
SUPT. TRANSPORTATION
ST. JOHN'S

(Author collection)

10   TIME TABLE NO. 27 — JUNE 17th, 1979

WESTWARD TRAINS					ST. JOHN'S SUBDIVISION			EASTWARD TRAINS		
THIRD CLASS	FOURTH CLASS	Miles from St. John's	Yard Limits			Office Signals	Siding Car Capacity	FOURTH CLASS	FOURTH CLASS	FOURTH CLASS
207 Mixed Monday Wednesday Friday	203 Freight Daily			Stations				204 Freight	208 Mixed	232 Mixed
1030	0630	0.0	↓ 4.0	ST. JOHN'S CKZ	HD	Yard	2130		1415
		7.3	6.5 8.0 ⟨	7.3 ST. ANNE Z		13			
1050	0655	8.8		1.5 IRVINE		48	2105		
f 1115	0720	19.1		10.3 KELLIGREWS		36	2035		f 1330
f 1140		30.1		11.0 HOLYROOD	HY	8	2010		f 1258
f 1155		36.2		6.1 AVONDALE	SC		1955		f 1241
f 1210	0820	41.6		5.4 Jct. with Carbonear Sub. BRIGUS JCT. *RY		36	1935		1230 s 0730
f 1225		49.1		7.5 OCEAN POND		36	1915		
s 1250	0905	54.5	54.1 35.2 ⟨	5.4 WHITBOURNE *RYZ	GO	7	1900	s 1615	0700
s 1305	0920	61.6	61.2 62.1 ⟨	7.1 Jct. with Argentia Sub. PLACENTIA JCT. *RZ			1835	s 1600	
To Argentia Sub-	0955	80.0		18.4 TICKLE HARBOUR		36	1750	From Argentia Sub-	
		97.7		17.7 FERGUSON		26	1710		
		110.2		12.5 GOOBIES Y	GB	29	1640		
	1145	131.1	130.6 ↑	20.9 CLARENVILLE CKZ	SO	51	1550		
				Rule 41 applicable Rule 105A not applicable			Daily	Monday Wednesday Friday	Tuesday Thursday Saturday
207	203						204	208	232

CNR passenger car logo (Author photo)

ST. JOHN'S 1964

Richard Manicom of Quebec City was determined to make his first visit to Newfoundland before starting his freshman year of university. Here, the 17-year-old catches CNR Train No. 1, the westbound *Caribou*, on August 12, 1964, just prior to her 16:30 summer schedule departure from the capital city. Here it is still mostly decorated in its handsome paint scheme of green and gold. The railway was in the middle of repainting the trains in the new image, black and light grey, as evidenced by the two cars farther back. With the termination of the passenger service just five years away, some would never see the new paint and finish their lives in the old colours. (Richard Manicom photo)

WATERFORD VALLEY 1984

Wanting to catch the last of the Newfoundland branch line mixed trains before termination, Kevin Day of Beaconsfield, QC, rides and shoots Terra Transport Mixed Extra 802 East from the rear coach returning from Argentia in July 1984. With only two months of service remaining, it is seen while making the grade crossing at Bay Bulls Road just south of the former Waterford Bridge Station. Once the junction for the 104-mile Trepassey Branch, it was reduced to a 13-car capacity siding in the 1950s and totally removed by the time this photo was taken. (Kevin Day photo)

BOWRING PARK 1955

On his only visit to Newfoundland, Sandy Goodrick of Mishawaka, Indiana, is fortunate to capture Mikado No. 326 heading Train No. 15, the westbound St. John's–Corner Brook first-class passenger express. Departing the capital city on Tuesdays, Thursdays, and Saturdays, it has just entered scenic Bowring Park on August 26, 1955, only two miles into its 405-mile journey. Delivered just six years earlier, on the eve of Confederation with Canada, the 326 would be scrapped by August of 1957, still practically brand new. Also in 1957, Nos. 15 and 16 would be discontinued on April 28 of that year, replaced instead by a daily year-round *Caribou* service. (Sandy Goodrick photo)

MOUNT PEARL 1984

While discovering his Newfoundland roots, Dan Rowsell of Victoria, BC, took some 21 rolls of film capturing hundreds of amazing narrow-gauge images across the Island. As observed from the coach on the mainline, the trainman carefully watches the trucks of CN boxcar 434025 being dropped from Mixed Extra 802 West to a customer on Riverview Avenue in Mount Pearl on August 12, 1984. The city within a city, Mount Pearl was unique in that the railway grade crossed two of its most recognizable streets, Commonwealth and Park Avenues, for all trains arriving or departing St. John's. (Dan Rowsell photo)

DONOVANS OVERPASS 1967

Wanting to make Centennial Year one to remember, John Freyseng of Ontario decided to travel with four University of Toronto friends and spouses all the way to Newfoundland to experience the island's rail passenger service. Here he captures CN Train No. 102, the eastbound *Caribou*, with lead NF210 No. 925 still wearing her as-delivered 1956 olive green and gold colours about to cross under the overpass at Donovans on June 22, 1967. The completion of the highway in 1965 necessitated the building of over a dozen such structures to eliminate all railway grade crossings while crossing Newfoundland by automobile. If adhering to schedule that day, the train should pull into the St. John's Station at 8:00 a.m., some 7.2 miles and 25 minutes away. (John Freyseng photo)

PARADISE 1984

Following a day of riding the mixed train to Carbonear and wanting to experience as much branch line railroading as possible, the photographer, with permission, boarded the lead engine of Terra Transport Mixed Extra 804 West for Argentia. Just a little more than a month away from discontinuance, it stops near St. Anne on August 13, 1984, to allow trainman Job Blackmore to pick up a mainland 40-foot boxcar while leaving the baggage and two coaches on the mainline during the switching. During this last full month of operations, Terra Transport often put on an additional coach to accommodate an increase in ridership. (Dan Rowsell photo)

MANUELS 1988

Having visited Newfoundland to photograph the island's trains in 1967, 1968, 1973, 1974, and 1982, Bill Linley of Ottawa returned once more, accompanied by his father, in 1988 to capture the last of operations just days before the official shutdown. After chasing this tiny train from Port aux Basques the day before, he shoots Extra 917 East at Manuels in Conception Bay South on September 27, 1988. NF210 No. 917 will soon return west to lead the last scheduled train from Bishop's Falls to Corner Brook three days later. Passenger service for Manuels ended on September 20, 1984, when Terra Transport Mixed Extra 804 East from Carbonear passed through the town for the last time. (Bill Linley photo)

LONG POND 1976

Interested in trains since childhood and photographing them in Britain, Europe, and North America, David Othen makes his way to Newfoundland to add to his portfolio. After shooting scenes in the St. John's yard and chasing the *Shoreline* the day before, it was now his turn to ride his first Newfoundland mixed train. While sitting in second unit G8 804 of CN Train No. 207, the Argentia Mixed, he looks back to capture G8 803, still in the old colours, with two boxcars, baggage, and coach at Long Pond on September 24, 1976. (David Othen photo, C. Robert Craig Memorial Library)

FOXTRAP 1984

Minus any freight cars, Terra Transport Mixed Extra 800 East, with a passenger-only consist, rounds the curve near the Foxtrap Marina and is now virtually at sea level. (A consist is a lineup or sequence of railroad carriages or cars, with or without a locomotive, that form a unit.) For the next 16 miles, this little train with two G8s, a baggage car, and three coaches will hug the waters of Conception Bay until turning inland at Woodfords west of Holyrood, thus giving it the name *Shoreline*. This location was once the site of the "Battle of Foxtrap" on June 26, 1880, when local residents, both men and women, armed with pitchforks, sticks, and rocks, stopped the surveying crew for fear of losing their land to the railway and a takeover by Canada. (Kevin Day photo)

KELLIGREWS 1967

As part of a special Centennial Year commemoration, James A. Brown, along with four University of Toronto friends and spouses, travelled to Newfoundland to ride and record the last of the islands passenger services. Following their arrival, they also took a day to chase the Carbonear Mixed and at this point caught up with her in Kelligrews, location of the famed Johnny Burke's *Kelligrews Soiree* folk song. On June 22, 1967, the eastbound mixed CN Train 232 with G8 801 in the lead follows the shore of Kelligrews Beach for a meet with the westbound freight 401 just ahead. (James A. Brown photo)

UPPER GULLIES 1976

Coach 757 brings up the rear of CN Mixed Train 232 at Upper Gullies en route to St. John's on September 23, 1976. Built in 1943 for the Newfoundland Railway as Coach No. 40, it served on both the *Overland Limited* and the *Caribou* but was later converted to branch line service by having an observation window for the conductor installed. The next day, the photographer and his wife would experience this ride themselves by travelling from St. John's to Holyrood, including a ride in the cab of G8 804 from St. Anne. (David Othen photo, C. Robert Craig Memorial Library)

SEAL COVE 1984
The shimmering blue waters of Conception Bay with Bell Island in the background make a beautiful backdrop for the Carbonear Mixed at Seal Cove on July 26, 1984. With G8s 805 and 804 producing a total of 1,750 horsepower, there would be no problem to climb the grade with the single 40-foot mainland boxcar and coach 757 in tow. Steve Patterson of Arvada, Colorado, made his only trip to Newfoundland in the summer of 1984 to ride and photograph the last narrow-gauge branch line mixed trains in North America and captured them in their fading glory for posterity. With less than two full months to go, scenes like this would become a distant memory. (Steve Patterson photo)

HOLYROOD 1967

A time-honoured tradition is captured from cabin car 6009 as the station agent is ready to hand over train orders to the conductor in baggage car 1308 of CN Mixed Train 232 at Holyrood on June 22, 1967. Originally built as steam generator car 2954 in 1956, it was converted to baggage car 1308 in 1964 at the St. John's shops. Having ridden the *Caribou* from Port aux Basques and wanting to experience a mixed train service for himself, the photographer boarded at Brigus Junction with the intention of a run to St. John's but disembarked at Holyrood instead to join his friends, including James A. Brown, in chasing the train the remaining 30 miles to the capital. (John Freyseng photo)

NORTH ARM 1967

Exiting the eastern portion of the massive horseshoe curve at North Arm in Holyrood Bay on June 22, 1967, CN Train No. 232 is returning from a run down the Carbonear Branch. Still wearing their original olive green and gold paint scheme as delivered in 1956, G8s 801, 800, and 804, products of GMD, were a common sight on the three branch lines then in operation. Built to replace the 4-6-2 Pacifics that operated on the Carbonear, Argentia, and Bonavista Branches, the 875-horsepower export model with the A-1-A trucks did a commendable job for over 28 years. (James A. Brown photo)

AVONDALE 1982

David Morris and fellow rail fans Fred Angus, George Patterson, and Bill Linley crossed the Gulf of St. Lawrence to spend a week in 1982 chasing and photographing every train operating on the island that year. Here the Fredericton, NB, native captures Train 231 coming to halt at Avondale for a sizable group of passengers en route to Carbonear on August 24, 1982. With three daily return trips a week out of St. John's since April 26, 1981, passenger patronage had increased significantly, and an extra coach was added. Avondale has the oldest surviving wooden station in Newfoundland and today is home to the Avondale Railway Station Museum. (David Morris photo)

BRIEN'S POND 1961

During the summer of 1961, 16-year-old Robert Coolidge travelled all the way from Boston to spend time with his Newfoundland relatives on the Bonavista Peninsula, and in the process, he captured many wonderful railway images. Leaning out of the coach, the teenager photographs CNR Train No. 1, the westbound *Caribou* climbing the grade at Brien's Pond just east of Brigus Junction wearing an all green and gold paint scheme in August of that year. The summer of 1961 saw major forest fires in the province, greatly hindering rail operations throughout the island and nearly causing him to miss his mainland connections. Despite this, the *Caribou* still managed to carry over 150,000 passengers that year. (Robert Coolidge photo)

BRIGUS JUNCTION OVERPASS 1978

Travelling with their families, Rich Taylor of Kearny, New Jersey, and his friend George Berisso spent a week photographing the unique narrow-gauge trains of New-foundland. Having just left Brigus Junction and assuming the new train number of 232, G8 800, with sisters 804, 801, and its consist of a single boxcar, baggage, and coach, is about to duck under the Trans-Canada Highway overpass just east of Brigus Junction on August 24, 1978. As one of only two such engines to retain that paint this late into the 1970s, it will be repainted in the CN zebra scheme before the decade is out. (Rich Taylor photo)

BRIGUS JUNCTION 1978

The photographer was pleasantly surprised to observe his very first narrow-gauge mixed train on the damp and drizzly day of August 23, 1978, when CN Train No. 207 suddenly appeared out of nowhere at Brigus Junction. Here he captures passengers entraining for the run to Argentia and all points in between. It would return here the next day as 208 after an overnight in Whitbourne, and obtaining a timetable from a friendly employee, the photographer and his friend would experience a ride to Carbonear and return themselves. Caboose 6071 was the second-last all welded steel one built in 1967 by National Steel Car (NSC) of Hamilton to replace the older wooden versions. (Rich Taylor photo)

OCEAN POND 1956

A young Robert J. Sandusky along with several other rail fans trekked from central Canada on an arranged trip to photograph and ride the last of mainline steam operations in the summer of 1956. Early in the morning, he catches the double-headed No. 2 *Caribou* hauled by 2-8-2 Mikado 310 and 4-6-2 Pacific 598 at Ocean Pond on June 20, 1956. The harsh Newfoundland winters required that snow fences be built at various flat open spaces along the route to help prevent the tracks from being covered in by drifts. With the arrival of 7 steam generator cars later that year, these beautiful engines would be replaced by some of the 35 new diesels already delivered. (Robert J. Sandusky photo)

WHITBOURNE 1982

A full-length CN Train 204 skirts the side of Junction Pond as it enters Whitbourne, Newfoundland's first inland town, on August 23, 1982. Having left Port aux Basques at noon the previous day, it is now 21.5 hours into its 24-hour journey to St. John's. The four diesel units, NF210s 945, 910, 936, and 930, head an equal combination of standard mainland boxcars and the newer 40-foot intermodal Terra Transport containers being introduced on the railway as a means of efficiency. From here to Placentia Junction was the only section on the St. John's subdivision that the *Caribou* passenger train could run at its maximum speed of 50 miles per hour. (David Morris photo)

ARGENTIA ACCESS OVERPASS 1984

With the Manual Block System now in effect, all trains were designated as "Extras" by the dispatcher, and thus the former CN Mixed Train 207 would now be designated as Terra Transport Mixed Extra 805 West as it approaches the Argentia Access Overpass on July 30, 1984. This is one of two places on the island where a connector road to the Trans-Canada Highway has a railway overpass on the mainline. This day's train was small with G8s 805 and 804, baggage 1308, and coach 757, and by September 19, 1984, the Argentia Mixed would make its final run. (Steve Patterson photo)

PLACENTIA JUNCTION 1984

Leaving the mainline at Placentia Junction, Terra Transport Mixed Extra 800 East is about to travel down the 20.7 miles to the ferry terminal at Argentia in July of 1984. Then the site of US Naval Station Argentia, the mixed train would require special access through the grounds of the American base. The track veering off to the right was where construction commenced to build the trans-island railway all the way to Port aux Basques in 1889, some 484 miles to the west. As evidenced by the work crew, the narrow-gauge track in Newfoundland was maintained to the highest standards, and crews took great pride in their work. (Kevin Day photo)

LONG HARBOUR 1982

Terra Transport Train 204 continues east at Long Harbour Station after crossing Route 202, the main road into the town, which grew as a result of the province's resettlement program of the 1960s. The visible siding here had a capacity for 20 cars, which were used by the former fluorspar plant ERCO. Immediately ahead of caboose 6069 is stock car 7076, which was placed to allow greater visibility for the caboose crews as the operating rules dictated. Sister stock car 7035 would survive to be part of a static narrow-gauge mixed train display at Exporail in Saint-Constant, QC. The caboose also survived to live another day, now being part of the Lewisporte Train Display. (Bill Linley photo)

TICKLE HARBOUR 1978

The late evening sun casts long shadows and is reflected on the side of the caboose at the tail end of CN Train No. 204 as it cruises through Tickle Harbour on August 25, 1978. Tickle Harbour was a flag stop on the isthmus of the Avalon Peninsula to serve communities such as Fair Haven, Placentia Bay, to the south and Bellevue, Trinity Bay, to the north until passenger service ended the morning of July 3, 1969. With the formation of Terra Transport in 1979, this is the last full year of 204 and its eastbound counterpart 203, as well as the various mixed trains on the branch lines referred to as "CN Train Number," later known as "Terra Transport Train Number." (Rich Taylor photo)

RANTEM 1984

While camping with his family and accessing a unique vantage point near the Doe Hills, the photographer was able to capture a rare shot of a full-length Terra Transport Extra 915 East approaching the former Rantem Station on July 11, 1984. With a wye (a triangular arrangement of three sections of railway track used for turning locomotives around) on the eastern side of the pond, as well as a water tower, Rantem was chosen as a site for one of the camps set up by the 1st Communications Squadron of the US Air Force in 1953, installing telegraph lines along the railway right of way. This freight, known less than two weeks earlier as 204 before the Manual Block System was implemented, had crossed under the Little Harbour Overpass on the Trans-Canada Highway seen in the background. (Robert J. Sandusky photo)

ISTHMUS OF AVALON 1984

On his one and only visit, computer engineer and international rail photographer Robert Palmer of Conshohocken, Pennsylvania, adds images of the Newfoundland narrow-gauge to his already prolific portfolio. Here he shoots Terra Transport Train No. 204 near La Manche Siding as it winds around the Precambrian rock of the Isthmus of Avalon, a narrow strip of barren, rocky land that connects the heavily populated Avalon Peninsula with the rest of Newfoundland, on June 19, 1984. This image is a great example of how close the railway ran along the more or less parallel Trans-Canada Highway, with the greatest gap being the 80-mile section between Badger and Deer Lake over the Gaff Topsails. (Robert Palmer photo)

SOUHERN HARBOUR 1984

As seen directly across from the entrance of Jack's Pond Provincial Park, NF210s 931, 925, and 941 lead Terra Transport Train 204 toward the station at Southern Harbour, Mileage 94.50, on June 19, 1984. Although no longer in service since the last passenger train in 1969, based on Timetable 80 from June 14, 1953, Southern Harbour Station was a flag stop for Train No. 1, the eastbound *Caribou*, on Wednesdays as well as the east- and westbound St. John's–Corner Brook express Nos. 15 and 16 and all freight trains. (Robert Palmer photo)

ARNOLD'S COVE 1953

Airman Jerome Young was assigned to the 1st Communications Construction Squadron of the US Air Force, responsible for installing new poles and anchors along the railway right of way as part of the Northeast Air Command. While waiting for orders from Canadian National Railways speeder operator Leroy Hawco, he captured the boxcar acting as a station, which replaced the original one burned by fire in 1934. In 1899, a train fare from St. John's to Arnold's Cove would set you back $3 if travelling first class and $2 via second class, while children's fare remained the same, that being half the price of an adult passenger. (Jerome Young photo, Merritt C. Scharnweber collection)

ARNOLD'S COVE OVERPASS 1984

Heading toward Arnold's Cove, Terra Transport Train 204 with caboose 6066 bringing up the rear has just passed underneath the fourth of many more railway overpasses constructed during the 1960s Trans-Canada Highway building boom. The slogan at the time was "We'll finish the drive in '65—thanks to Mr. Pearson!" Ironically, it was the completion of the Trans-Canada Highway that spelled the beginning of the end for the island's passenger train service only four years later. (Robert Palmer photo)

COME BY CHANCE 1984

When one talks of the unique place names of Newfoundland and Labrador, Come By Chance is usually at the top of the list, and perhaps it inspired the photographer to chase a train there on June 19, 1984. With that, Terra Transport Train No. 204 continues the journey toward the provincial capital that day, carrying, among the consist, 6 of the 45 40-ton longitudinal hoppers built in 1958 and 1959 for the Canadian National Railways. Just east of this point is a spur line and a wye that was built to service the Come by Chance oil refinery when it opened in 1973. (Robert Palmer photo)

GOOBIES 1982

With the signal indicating clear, and brake smoke in the background, Terra Transport Train 204 is about to pass the station at Goobies at the permitted speed of 30 miles per hour on August 26, 1982. Directly behind NF210s 940, 941, and 921 are idling G8s 800 and 802, which were picked up in Clarenville for a routine inspection in St. John's. Named after sawmill owner George Goobie, the station in Goobies, like most along the line from St. John's to Port aux Basques, would close its doors for good two years later in September of 1984. (David Morris photo)

GOOBIES OVERPASS 1984

Looking westward from the Goobies Overpass while waiting for the arrival of Terra Transport Train No. 204, it is quite obvious that the 1,675-foot, 36-car capacity siding has not been regularly used in some time. Situated over Route 210, the Heritage Run, it is one of the two mainline overpasses on a connector road to the Trans-Canada Highway. Just east was a wye that was still in service at the time this photo was taken, part of the original proposed 102-mile Fortune Bay Branch commenced in 1915. With 43 miles of track laid to Terrenceville, it was never operated and was dismantled in 1939. (Robert Palmer photo)

TUNNEL 1952

Omer Lavallée of Quebec made two trips in the 1950s to capture the last of steam operations in Canada's newest province. While travelling with his friend and fellow rail fan Ron Ritchie on Canadian National Railways Train No. 2, the eastbound *Caribou*, he photographed the tiny flag stop of Tunnel on June 25, 1952, from the sleeper *Buchans*, the last car on the rear. At Milepost 121.93, it was the location of the twenty-first water chute (operated by hauling the pipe into the locomotive's tender) encountered since leaving Port aux Basques the previous day. (Omer Lavallée photo)

Train 203 in Gander, August 27, 1982 (David Morris photo)

CHAPTER 2

CLARENVILLE SUBDIVISION

TERRA TRANSPORT
TIME TABLE

101

EFFECTIVE TUESDAY, JUNE 1ST, 1982

REFER TO PAGE 1 FOR EFFECTIVE TIME, AND FOR
OTHER TIME AND DATE CHANGES THAT WILL OCCUR

THE SUPERIOR DIRECTION IS EAST OR SOUTH

*SAFETY IS OF THE FIRST IMPORTANCE
IN THE DISCHARGE OF DUTY*

P.A. CLARKE
PRESIDENT AND GENERAL MANAGER
ST. JOHN'S

A.N. PENNEY
SUPT. TRANSPORTATION
ST. JOHN'S

(Author collection)

TIME TABLE NO. 101 - JUNE 1st, 1982

WESTWARD TRAINS				CLARENVILLE SUBDIVISION	Office Signals	Siding Capacity in Feet	EASTWARD TRAINS	
FOURTH CLASS 203 Freight Daily Except Saturday	Miles from St. John's	Yard Limits		Stations			FOURTH CLASS 204 Freight	
0210	131.1			CLARENVILLE ... CKYZ	SO	Yard	0620	
		↓		1.1 Jct. with Bonavista Sub.				
	132.2			SHOAL HARBOUR				
		132.9		4.3				
	136.5			STANLEY		2396		
				6.9				
	143.4			THORBURN LAKE		2552		
				7.5				
0250	150.9			PORT BLANDFORD		1470	0535	
				13.7				
	164.6			TERRA NOVA	AN	2617		
				16.5				
0430	181.1			ALEXANDER BAY	AB	2685	0430	
				9.0				
	190.1			GAMBO	GS	1184		
				14.1				
	204.2			BENTON		1942		
				8.7				
0540	212.9	212.2 217.0		GANDER ... YZ	AP	2079	0320	
		229.4		17.4				
	230.3	231.0		GLENWOOD ... YZ	GW	1866		
				14.2				
0645	244.5	243.9 245.1		NOTRE DAME ... YZ	NO	2038	0215	
				11.8				
	256.3			RATTLING		3276		
				11.0				
0730	267.3	266.4 ↑		BISHOPS FALLS ... CKZ	BF	Yard	0130	
203				Rule 41 applicable Rule 105A not applicable			Daily Except Saturday 204	

Narrow-gauge freight cars in Clarenville, August 26, 1978 (Rich Taylor photo)

CLARENVILLE 1977

After leaving his job in Tulsa, Oklahoma, to visit Newfoundland, Paul Enenbach managed to ride two of the four mixed trains still operating in 1977 and made a lifetime of memories. Just before boarding the coach on CN Train No. 206, he captured the engineer getting ready to move G8s 805 and 800, the first and last of the series, to the front of the Bonavista mixed on June 1, 1977. Six export model G8s were built in 1956, with narrow-gauge trucks, by GMD of London, Ontario, after the Canadian National Railways considered the General Electric 70-tonner for branch line use and an unsuccessful trial of the three GE 380-horsepower centre-cab units already on the roster since 1948. (Paul Enenbach photo)

SHOAL HARBOUR JUNCTION 1982

Terra Transport Mixed Train 206 with G8s 800 and 802 as head end power is leaving the mainline at Shoal Harbour, Mileage 132.2, for the 88-mile run down the longest operating branch line remaining. In addition to the boxcar and flat, coach 754 and caboose 6061 made up the consist on August 25, 1982. This line would be officially closed on June 20, 1984, but G8 802 would be the lead engine on the last run when the track was closed for safety reasons on November 23, 1983, never to see a train again. (David Morris photo)

SHOAL HARBOUR OVERPASS 1982

An unusual shot of what appears to be a mixed train east of Bishop's Falls on August 26, 1982. The coach at the tail end of Terra Transport Train 204 was not part of its normal consist. Routinely dropped at Bishop's Falls as part of the consist from Corner Brook as a mixed, coach 760 would now be dropped at nearby Clarenville and attached to the westbound 203. Built by the Canadian Car & Foundry in 1943 as coach 43 for the Newfoundland Railway under the lend-lease agreement, its number was changed to 760 after takeover by the Canadian National Railways. (David Morris photo)

RIOUX 1958
While the Trans-Canada Highway was being constructed across the new province, there were still some major gaps to fill by rail before its completion in 1965. The Canadian National Railways put on a dedicated train ferry service that first ran from Gander to Clarenville and later from Gambo to Clarenville with a single diesel, a dozen or so flatcars, and a coach or two at the rear to accommodate drivers and passengers. While travelling across Newfoundland with his family, Richard Stoker captured this rare colour shot of the CNR train ferry on July 3, 1958, at Rioux, destined for Gambo. (Stoker Family Fonds, Maritime History Archive photo)

THORBOURNE LAKE OVERPASS 1984
Suddenly appearing out of the woods, Terra Transport Extra 941 East is about to duck under the Thorbourne Lake Overpass on July 25, 1984. The train has just finished climbing one of the railway's longest and steepest grades. Back in the days of steam, engines taking water at South West, several miles west, would have to back up to make a run for the hill. This downward-looking shot gives an excellent view of the tops of NF210s 941, 940, 934, and 911. (Steve Patterson photo)

PORT BLANDFORD 1980

Travelling to Newfoundland for a vacation in 1980 with a university buddy, John Eull managed to find some time to photograph trains on his only trip to the province. Here he captures a full-length Terra Transport 204 rumbling along Clode Sound through the town of Port Blandford on June 16, 1980. Port Blandford was the terminus for the SS *Dundee*, which served communities on the Bonavista Peninsula. The Newfoundland Railway steamer would leave every Monday after the arrival of Trains No. 1 and 2 with passengers, mail, and cargo until the opening of the Bonavista Branch in 1911. (John Eull photo)

PORT BLANDFORD OVERPASS 1982

At the eastern boundary of Terra Nova National Park, Terra Transport Train 204 is about to ride under yet another Trans-Canada Highway overpass while running four hours late on a grey and rainy August 26, 1982. The photographer and his friends would continue to chase and photograph this train at several locations as far as Holyrood before nightfall. With one of the few gaps where the railway does not parallel the TCH, the rails have not been seen from the highway since just outside of Alexander Bay Station, some 30 miles to the west. (Bill Linley photo)

TERRA NOVA 1953

Airman Merritt B. Scharnweber of the USAF 1st Communications Squadron is seen on the speeder approaching the freshly painted double span truss bridge at Terra Nova in the summer of 1953. Their workday of installing new poles and anchors along the route is only just beginning. With takeover of the Newfoundland Railway by the Canadian National Railways only four years earlier, new signs were installed along the route, not only identifying specific locations but also promoting "Courtesy & Service" by Canadian National Railways. (Jerome Young photo, Merritt B. Scharnweber collection)

TERRA NOVA NATIONAL PARK 1988

Air Canada pilot and rail fan Steve Bradley travelled to the island to record on film and video the last days of the Newfoundland Railway. As Terra Transport Extra 944 East, the last scheduled eastbound freight, skirted the western boundary of Terra Nova National Park, engineer Munroe Greening conducted a run past for the photographer on September 29, 1988. Soon the five-unit train with two gondolas of scrap and a caboose would arrive at the end of the subdivision in Clarenville, and Monroe would sign off for the last time while Steve would ride as far as Whitbourne. To quote the photographer, "Riding the last official train east from Bishop's Falls to St. John's was probably the most emotional trip I have ever ridden." (Steve Bradley photo)

ALEXANDER BAY STATION 1952

Still wearing the red Newfoundland Railway colours of her predecessor, Canadian National Railways Train No. 2, the eastbound *Caribou* with 2-8-2 Mikado No. 300, stops at Alexander Bay Station on June 26, 1952, to entrain and detrain passengers. In typical fashion on the island, the siding ran behind the station. This station was located high on a ridge and built to serve communities on the Eastport Peninsula with all goods and services for the Glovertown area going through there. Before long, Newfoundland Railway red on the coaches, diners, and sleepers would soon give way to the CNR olive green. (Omer Lavallée photo)

GAMBO OVERPASS 1988

Famed photographer Charlie Falk of Gander spent a considerable amount of time shooting the last two months of rail operations on the island. Here he captured Terra Transport Extra 938 East approaching the Trans-Canada Highway overpass on September 19, 1988, with NF210 sisters 928, 924, and 936, all wearing the newer Terra Transport bidirectional arrow scheme. Nearby at Mileage 188.50 was the wye and spur to Gambo Pond, an important pulpwood loading area for the Anglo-Newfoundland Development Company, once the largest employer in the area. Just eleven days later, Charlie would chase and shoot the very last westbound mixed freight. (Charlie Falk photo)

GAMBO 1975

Canadian Pacific engineer and rail photographer Phil Mason of Kamloops, BC, travelled much of the country in May of 1975, eventually finding his way to Newfoundland, where he chased and photographed nearly all trains running that year. Deciding to shoot at locations with interesting place names, he caught Canadian National Train No. 204 running eastward through Gambo on May 10, 1975, with the quadrant signal in the down position. Lead engine 907 is one of nine of the NF110 1,200-horsepower road switchers built by GMD for the CNR's Newfoundland division from 1952 to 1953. A wreck at Gambo Side Hill on May 17, 1951 was one of Newfoundland's worst, when steam engines 1017 and 305 derailed, killing engineer Ted Stanley and seriously injuring fireman Frank Cole. (Phil Mason photo)

BENTON 1967

Canadian National mechanical engineer Conrad Steeves was travelling in business car No. 3 on the tail end of mixed freight 203 en route to Port aux Basques in Canada's Centennial Year when he captured a three-way meet at Benton on June 30, 1967. To the right is daily eastbound scheduled freight No. 400, which occupied the passing track and moved forward to allow the westbound daily mixed 203 to move ahead on the mainline. With the canopy of the business car framing the picture, in the background, westbound *Caribou* No. 101 holds the mainline until 203 can run safely ahead. Business car No. 3 was only one of three such cars on the roster at the time, the others being *Avalon* and *Terra Nova*. (Conrad Steeves photo)

GANDER 1967

In this early morning scene at Gander, the trainman waits to throw the switch so that Canadian National Freight 209, the Lewisporte–Gander fuel train, can enter the mainline at Gander on June 23, 1967. With Gander being the "Crossroads of the World" for aviation, this fuel train ran daily from Monday to Friday to keep the airport supplied for the hundreds of transatlantic flights landing monthly. As viewed from CN Train 101, the westbound *Caribou*, the single locomotive on 209 is NF210 No. 946, the last of the series. Built and delivered by GMD of London, ON, in January of 1960, it had a class of GR-12x and was still wearing its original green and gold paint scheme. (James A. Brown photo)

GLENWOOD OVERPASS 1975

Heading out from under the Trans-Canada Highway overpass at Glenwood, Canadian National Train No. 204 continues eastward with three of its four units on a sunny May 10, 1975. All products of GMD of London, ON, lead unit NF110 907 was built in 1953, while NF210 sisters 919 and 943 were products from 1956 and 1960 respectively. During the building of the TCH, in order to avoid grade crossings for safety, a total of 18 overpasses were constructed, including one over the Carbonear Branch. (Phil Mason photo)

GLENWOOD 1980

On one of his multiple trips to Newfoundland from 1977 to 1984, Joe McMillan, former Santa Fe Railway employee and now owner of McMillan Publications, shoots Terra Transport Extra 931 West with caboose 6063 waiting for departure from the tiny station at Glenwood on July 31, 1980. For many years, the Bowater Paper Mill in Corner Brook was one of the biggest customers of the railway with pulpwood cut in the central Newfoundland region being shipped on dedicated pulpwood trains. As indicated by the sign on the station, this was also a scheduled stop for the daily CN/Terra Transport RoadCruiser bus, which replaced the trans-island passenger service in 1969. (Joe McMillan photo)

NOTRE DAME JUNCTION 1982

Station agent Gerald Dwyer has just handed up the orders for westbound Canadian National Train No. 203 to trainman Wilson Butt for them to meet eastbound counterpart 204 at Rattling. The track in the foreground is the 9.4-mile spur to Lewisporte, which in the 1953 Timetable No. 80 saw as many as eight trains a day except for Sundays, all of them mixed to connect with mainline passenger trains Nos. 1,2, 15, and 16, as well as the daily freights and way freights. Agent Dwyer, who was also the only Newfoundlander to score a goal against Boston Bruins goaltender Terry Sawchuk, worked at the station from 1964 until its closing in 1984, the longest of any agent since its establishment in 1898. (David Morris photo)

NORRIS ARM 1975

Travelling with fellow rail fan and friend Phil Mason, Stan J. Smaill of Montreal, on his first of two trips to the island, they begin chasing Canadian National Train No. 204 from Bishop's Falls eastward toward St. John's on May 10, 1975. Shooting from what is now the former Trans-Canada Highway, he captured lead engine NF110 907 with NF210 919 about to pass Our Lady of Mount Carmel Roman Catholic Church, and with those two engines plus 923 and 947, the rumble of 4,800 horsepower would break the quiet stillness of that Saturday morning. (Stan J. Smaill photo)

RATTLING 1982

Following orders received at Notre Dame Junction, Terra Transport 203 holds the 67-car siding to allow eastbound 204 with engines 945, 910, and 937 to continue along the mainline on August 27, 1982. Upon arrival at Bishop's Falls, coach 760 picked up at Clarenville will be marshalled to the rear of 203 for the run to Corner Brook, thus making that train then Terra Transport Mixed 203 over the entire Bishop's Falls Subdivision. The lengthy siding was installed in 1966 to replace the two shorter sidings at Norris Arm and Jumpers Brook. (David Morris photo)

EXPLOITS RIVER OVERPASS 1976

Mike McIlwaine of Ridgetown Ontario, and three friends made a trip in May of 1976 to photograph railways in New Brunswick, Nova Scotia, and Newfoundland. He caught Canadian National Train No. 204 approaching the overpass located just south of the Sir Robert Bond Bridge over the Exploits River and the longest highway bridge anywhere on the Trans-Canada Highway. With a friendly wave from the engineer of lead unit 942, sisters 941 and 939 bring the heavily laden freight up to track speed en route to Jumpers Brook. The three NF210 units were collectively in the final order of an additional nine diesels delivered in 1960. (Mike McIlwaine photo, Brad Jolliffe collection)

EXPLOITS BRIDGE 1984

Running cab forward, which was not standard operating practice in Newfoundland, the Lewisporte Switcher as Terra Transport Extra 946 East is caught crossing the Exploits Bridge with its maximum speed of 10 miles per hour on August 1, 1984. With the town of Bishop's Falls in the background, the 927-foot Exploits Bridge was completed in 1901 by Dominion Bridge Company to replace three that were all washed away by ice about half a mile below this location. The longest railway bridge on the Island, it was built on abutments of granite from Quarry in the Gaff Topsails. (Steve Patterson photo)

Mixed Extra 933 West at Millertown Junction, August 1988 (Stan J. Smaill photo)

CHAPTER 3

BISHOP'S FALLS SUBDIVISION

TerraTransport
TIME TABLE

106

EFFECTIVE SUNDAY, MAY 1st, 1988

REFER TO PAGE 1 FOR EFFECTIVE TIME, AND FOR
OTHER TIME AND DATE CHANGES THAT WILL OCCUR

*SAFETY IS OF THE FIRST IMPORTANCE
IN THE DISCHARGE OF DUTY*

J.H. EASTON
PRESIDENT AND GENERAL MANAGER
ST. JOHN'S

R.J. WALSH
SUPT. TRANSPORTATION
ST. JOHN'S

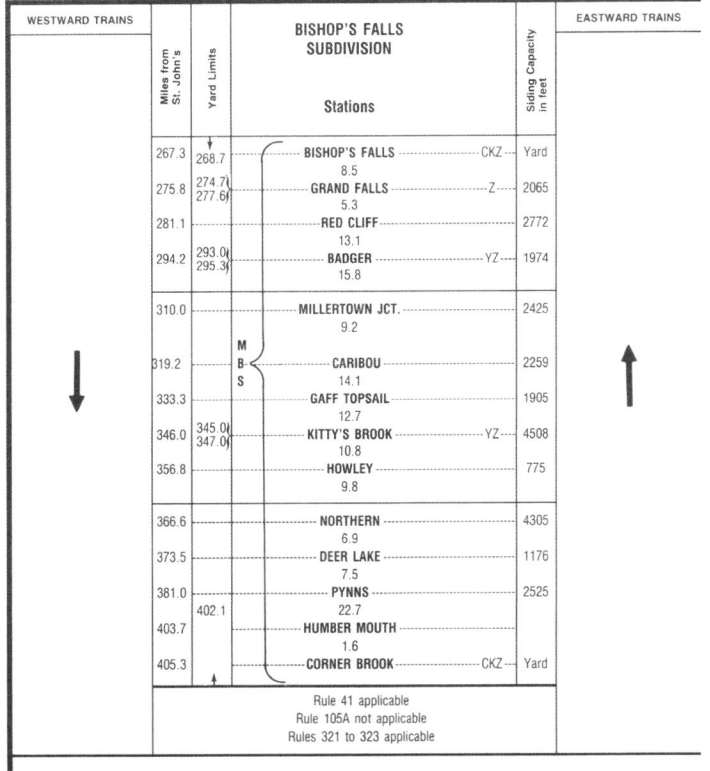

WESTWARD TRAINS	Miles from St. John's	Yard Limits	BISHOP'S FALLS SUBDIVISION Stations	Siding Capacity in feet	EASTWARD TRAINS
	267.3	268.7	BISHOP'S FALLS ——— CKZ	Yard	
			8.5		
	275.8	274.7 277.6	GRAND FALLS ——— Z	2065	
			5.3		
	281.1		RED CLIFF	2772	
			13.1		
	294.2	293.0 295.3	BADGER ——— YZ	1974	
			15.8		
	310.0		MILLERTOWN JCT.	2425	
			9.2		
	319.2	M B S	CARIBOU	2259	
			14.1		
	333.3		GAFF TOPSAIL	1905	
			12.7		
	346.0	345.0 347.0	KITTY'S BROOK ——— YZ	4508	
			10.8		
	356.8		HOWLEY	775	
			9.8		
	366.6		NORTHERN	4305	
			6.9		
	373.5		DEER LAKE	1176	
			7.5		
	381.0		PYNNS	2525	
			22.7		
	403.7	402.1	HUMBER MOUTH		
			1.6		
	405.3		CORNER BROOK ——— CKZ	Yard	

Rule 41 applicable
Rule 105A not applicable
Rules 321 to 323 applicable

(Author collection)

Interior of Mixed Train Coach 764, April 16, 1988 (Author photo)

BISHOP'S FALLS 1969
Upon learning that the trans-island passenger train *Caribou* was on the verge of imminent cancellation, newly married Doug Leffler of Michigan and his bride, Sandy, rushed to Newfoundland in April of 1969 to experience a last ride for themselves. Leaning out of the vestibule for much of his return journey, he managed to shoot some wonderful images as seen from the train. While at Bishop's Falls for its scheduled 20-minute stop on April 25, 1969, he captured westbound Canadian National Train No. 101 before reboarding the drawing room of the sleeper *Whitbourne*. No doubt the young air cadets would stir up memories for the older gentlemen by the station, of when the island was occupied by Canadian and American servicemen during World War II. (Doug Leffler photo)

BISHOP'S FALLS OVERPASS 1977

In search of a narrow-gauge engine for Pinafore Park in St. Thomas, Ontario, Larry Broadbent and companions travelled to Newfoundland to see what was available in September of 1977. With a focus on the recently closed ASARCO railway of Buchans and the GFCR of Botwood, he was able to photograph some mainline images during his time. With the white flags flying, designating it as an "Extra," NF210 910 running cab forward and caboose 6069 are about to dip under the overpass downgrade from Cruisers in September 1977. The 910 was the second in an order of 26 NF210s built in 1956 by GMD and delivered direct from Montreal to St. John's on the SS *Christen Smith* to forever banish the 2-8-2 Mikado and 4-6-2 Pacific steam engines. (Larry Broadbent photo)

CRUISERS 1988

Terra Transport Mixed Extra 935 West has just crossed under the Trans-Canada Highway overpass in Bishop's Falls on April 16, 1988, and is climbing upgrade at Cruisers Brook, said to be the steepest grade on the entire 547-mile Newfoundland Railway. Departing Bishop's Falls at 11:00 a.m., the two NF210s (935 and 927) leave with passenger-only equipment (baggage 1308 and coach 764) until four container units were picked up in Grand Falls. The only travellers to make the entire 138-mile journey to Corner Brook were the author and his friend Paul, who was delighted to experience his first ride on a Newfoundland train. One other, a cabin owner, got on at Millertown Junction and soon departed in several feet of snow at Gaff Topsail. The hospitality and friendliness of the Newfoundland crews went above and beyond, with conductor Carl Dillon inviting us both back to the caboose and allowing us to ride in the cupola. (Author photo)

GRAND FALLS 1952

Eastbound Canadian National Railways Fourth Class Freight No. 52, with mostly narrow-gauge outside braced boxcars in the consist, prepares to leave Grand Falls with single Mikado 2-8-2 No. 316 on the head end on June 28, 1952. Built in 1944 by the American Locomotive Company (ALCO) of Schenectady, New York, as No. 1016 for the Newfoundland Railway, after takeover by the CNR it was renumbered 316 with a class of 2R-2-C and would remain on the roster service until scrapping in August of 1957. Grand Falls was also the headquarters of the private industrial line 22-mile Grand Falls Central Railway, whose main purpose was the movement of newsprint to the port in Botwood for overseas shipping. (Omer Lavallée photo)

RED CLIFF OVERPASS 1968

Ted Wickson of Toronto, along with fellow rail fans Bill Linley and Terry Thompson, spent an incredible ten-day adventure shooting everything on the roster and time-table in October of 1968. Chasing Canadian National Mixed Train No. 203 with two baggage cars and coach 761 in front of caboose 6057, he caught up with it on October 9, 1968, just passing under the Red Cliff Overpass, continuing to its next stop at Badger. Only eight days before, CN had terminated railway post office (RPO) cars on 203 and 204, which had been assigned to the trans-island mixed trains since being removed from the *Caribou* in 1958. At the time of this photo, it would take the 203 just shy of 30 hours to cross the island. (Ted Wickson photo)

BADGER 1976

Canadian National Extra 938 East crosses the Badger River on May 6, 1976, en route to Bishop's Falls with a load of ore from the ASARCO mine in Buchans. Due to the geographic isolation, it would take three railways to transport the ore from Buchans to shipping at Botwood. The ASARCO trains hauled it the 37 miles to Millertown Junction, where it was then transported a further 43 miles to Bishop's Falls on the CN mainline. From there the GFCR took it the remaining 12 miles to Botwood on their own private line. Just over a year later, on June 29, 1977, the last load of ore was carried over the CN line by Extra 939 East. The Trans-Canada Highway would be not seen again until 80 miles west at Deer Lake. (Mike McIlwaine photo, Brad Jollife collection)

MILLERTOWN JUNCTION 1969

As observed from the vestibule of the sleeper *Whitbourne*, westbound *Caribou* No. 101 makes a scheduled stop at Millertown Junction on April 25, 1969. Named for the ANDCo. Millertown Railway (and later the Buchans Railway) Junction with the then Newfoundland Railway mainline, the sidings and other tracks here had a total capacity for 122 cars. It was only connected by road two years earlier, in 1967, from the Buchans Highway, and up until then, the only access to this remote town was by train. If keeping with the schedule, the time should be 11:10 a.m., and before long, folks will be heading to the diner for some of the finest meals anywhere on the island and expertly served by dedicated stewards such as Ned Hunt and others. (Doug Leffler photo)

CARIBOU 1978

Nearing the end of the long siding at Caribou, the photographer turns to shoot former Canadian National caboose 6049 on August 28, 1978. This car was built in St. John's in 1957 using the frame of former Newfoundland Railway flatcar 1831, which was built in 1938. With the arrival of the 20 steel cabooses from 1961 to 1967, it was no longer required and sold in 1971. It was then moved by a work train to this location and used as a hunting camp. Caribou was also the site chosen to commemorate the very last scheduled train when Terra Transport Mixed Extra 917 West stopped on September 30, 1988, for crew pictures and a cake decorated in the shape of a train. (Rich Taylor photo)

MARY MARCH 1978

As observed from the cupola of the caboose, Canadian National Train 203 Mixed is nearly finished crossing the single span truss bridge over Mary March Brook. The details of the top of the coach in front are quite visible while a work crew performs maintenance on the left side of the bridge over the brook named for Mary March. This was the English name given to Demasduit, a Beothuk woman who was taken captive by Englishman John Peyton Jr. in 1819. Mary March was also the location of a wye and huge shed that held coal and the railway's rotary plow, two steam engines, three tenders, and a cookhouse/bunkhouse when not clearing snow. (Rich Taylor photo)

QUARRY 1988

Train service was dwindling by the time of this photo in late August 1988, down to just three mixed runs a week, but was still utilized by hunters, berry pickers, and cabin owners in the Gaff Topsails region. Terra Transport Mixed Extra 933 West stops at Quarry to entrain two berry pickers near the spur that was built at Mileage 325 to drop a former White Fleet work car as a cabin. Originally built in 1943 by Canadian Car and Foundry (CC&F) for the Newfoundland Railway as the sleeper *Buchans*, it kept the name and was numbered No. 302 by the CNR but was converted to work car 5023 in 1973. Quarry was the site of a large granite deposit that was used to build the Victorian Era station as headquarters for the Newfoundland Railway in 1903, and it also provided cobblestones for Water Street in St. John's. The station was reclassified as unmanned by the Canadian National Railways in 1954. (Stan J. Smaill photo)

SUMMIT 1978

A lengthy Canadian National Train No. 203 Mixed with mostly empty 40-foot steel boxcars and flatcars returning to the mainland is about to crest Summit on August 28, 1978. At 1,554 feet above sea level, it is the highest point of the railway across the entire island. The four Topsail mountains—Gaff, Main, Mizzen, and Fore, named after the masts on a sailing ship—are all visible from this location. Just west of Summit, all trains run downgrade to Howley, some 28 miles away. It was the decision to build the railway over the Gaff Topsails shorter route, which cost so much in terms of snow clearing and maintenance, that negated any savings by avoiding the longer route north toward Halls Bay. (George Berisso photo)

GAFF TOPSAILS 1984

Enveloped in brake shoe smoke, Terra Transport Extra 910 West grinds to a halt at Gaff Topsail on August 1, 1984, to entrain two passengers destined for points west of a place name cemented in Newfoundland railway lore. The mixed portion of the former 203 owes its existence to the fact that several communities not yet connected to the newly completed Trans-Canada Highway would not have any means of access to the outside with the cancellation of the *Caribou* in 1969. Therefore, the Canadian Transport Commission recommended that a coach be added to the daily east- and westbound freights between Badger and Deer Lake. The little yellow cabin once belonged to roadmaster J. T. Hannon but now is in the hands of Brad Lingard, son of former railroader turned author and historian, Mont Lingard. (Steve Patterson photo)

POND CROSSING 1967

Canadian National Train No. 101, the *Caribou*, winds around several turns after leaving Pond Crossing on June 20, 1967, while still climbing upgrade on the western side of the Gaff Topsails. The setting sun on one of the longest days of the year shows all cars ahead of the photographer painted in the new post-1961 black and light grey scheme. With arrival at Gaff Topsail scheduled for 18:40 and about a mile away, many have finished up a delicious meal in diner 173 and, according to the photographer, will spend several delightful hours being entertained in diner/café car 172 at the head end. (John Freyseng photo)

KITTY'S BROOK 1987

Upon learning from a Terra Transport engineering friend that a mixed train was operating over the Bishop's Falls Subdivision, the author and his girlfriend rushed to Bishop's Falls to take their first Newfoundland train ride. Terra Transport Mixed Extra 945 West is seen here downgrade at Kitty's Brook east as the spring runoff under the trestle is quite evident on April 20, 1987. They were the only passengers in coach 757 for the entire 138-mile journey from Bishop's Fall to Corner Brook that day. Kitty's Brook had not only a wye to turn plow trains around but also a fallout shelter constructed during the 1950s bomb paranoia. (Author photo)

HOWLEY 1988

As seen from the second unit, NF210 915, engineer Joseph Hickey expertly brings Terra Transport Mixed Extra 933 West to a stop at Howley to entrain some passengers in August of 1988. Named after geologist and surveyor James P. Howley, whose maps and surveys were essential for the building of the railway, it was one of the towns not accessible by any road in 1969, thus one of the reasons the Canadian Transport Commission ordered that a mixed run be maintained. Howley was also the site of the introduction of moose to the island when four transported by boxcar from Chatham, New Brunswick, were released here in 1904. The 915, along with 917, was one of two diesels to have the experimental Terra Transport paint scheme applied in 1979 with a small arrow and black cab. With 917 being repainted in the later scheme, the 915 remained a unique locomotive until the end. (Stan J. Smaill photo)

HOWLEY BRIDGE 1958

With a particular interest in narrow-gauge railways, World War II Canadian Army veteran John D. Knowles of Toronto made four trips to Newfoundland from 1952 to 1958, travelling the entire line to record the transition from steam to full dieselization. As seen from the last sleeper on the rear of the now diesel-hauled *Caribou* No. 1, the westbound train has just crossed the Howley lift bridge on August 4, 1958, complete with another tidy white Canadian National Railways "Courtesy & Service" location sign. This bridge was the site of a permanent timetable "stop and proceed" slow movement, where at times tugboats would run through the lifted trestle between Sandy and Grand Lake. (John D. Knowles photo)

GRAND LAKE 1988

A common sight during the summer of 1988 was the passenger consist of coach 764, baggage 1308, and coach 757 on the rear of the tri-weekly mixed train between Bishop's Falls and Corner Brook. Normally the mixed only carried one coach, but with the announcement made about the impending shutdown, an extra was added for those wishing to take a last ride. On this day, Terra Transport Mixed Extra 933 West crosses the causeway over Newfoundland's largest lake with that very same consist in addition to the dozen or so 40-foot flats carrying the green intermodal containers. Earlier in the year, coach 764 and baggage 1308 were fully refurbished at the St. John's shops for the new mixed train schedule commencing in April, following a Canadian Transport Commission decision to continue the service after a winter shutdown but at a reduced frequency. (Stan J. Smaill photo)

MAIN DAM 1962
Montreal-born Doug Robinson was able to record some wonderful images of Newfoundland rail operations when visiting his grandparents in Howley in the early 1960s. One of these included this forward shot taken from the nose of the leading diesel of an extra westbound pulpwood freight with the chutes open on Main Dam at Mileage 364.3 in August 1962. The 244-metre-long and 24-metre-high Ambursen-type structure, built in 1924 to provide electricity to the new paper mill in Corner Brook, backed up water on Grand Lake some 130 kilometres. The resulting flooding required an 17.7-kilometre diversion from Howley to Intake, fully paid for by the Newfoundland Pulp and Paper Company. (Doug Robinson photo)

NORTHERN 1967
As seen from the sleeper *Clarenville* of the eastbound *Caribou* No. 102, engineer John Dicks takes westbound No. 203 mixed out from the lengthy siding at Northern on June 20, 1967, now that the passenger train is clear. One of the longest sidings on the Bishop's Falls Subdivision, it had a capacity for 52 cars. The tail end of 203 that day included not only a rare centre cupola caboose but also two baggage cars and a railway post office car. Once part of the head end consist of the *Caribou*, RPOs were reassigned to new freights No. 3 and No. 4 in 1958. This would also be their last full year of service on the mixed freights, as they would be discontinued in October of 1968 with the mail being transferred to trucks. (John Freyseng photo)

HUMBER CANAL 1962

As photographed by his nephew, proud engineer Lester Faulkner of Canadian National Railways Extra 909 West with trailing unit NF110 904 is captured in front of his pulpwood train at Humber Canal in August of 1962. This was a special siding where loads of bundled pulpwood, and later stacked pulpwood, were carried on dedicated trains from Glenwood and dropped into the waters of the Humber Canal. From there they would enter and float down a chute into Deer Lake until collected by tugs at the mouth of the Humber River for the Bowater paper mill in Corner Brook. Lead unit 909 was the first of the new series designated NF210 to distinguish them from their NF110 brethren and built in a batch of 26 by GMD that were delivered to Newfoundland in 1956. (Doug Robinson photo)

DEER LAKE 1977

Trailing four units and with plumes of diesel exhaust filling the air, NF110 903 rushes Canadian National Mixed Train No. 203 past boxcar 567363 through the community of Deer Lake on June 5, 1977. The 37-car train with a single coach on the rear didn't stop that day but went straight on to Corner Brook, where the coach would be dropped for the return journey that evening on No. 204. (Paul Enenbach photo)

DEER LAKE OVERPASS 1988

Terra Transport Mixed Extra 940 West with units 941 and 944, a depressed centre flat, regular flat, two coaches, baggage, and caboose is about to pass under the Trans-Canada Highway overpass after crossing the Humber Canal spillway in Deer Lake on September 21, 1988. This is the first encounter with the mostly parallel TCH since last leaving it behind at Badger, some 80 miles due east. Amazingly, all three engines have survived. The 940 is on static display at Whitbourne, Newfoundland, while sister 941 was sold to F.C. del Pacifico of Nicaragua and 944 to F.C. Antofagasta Boliva of Chile. (Omer Lavallée photo)

SOUTH BROOK 1982

NF210 units 921, 930, 938, 918, and 936 head Canadian National Mixed Train No. 203 with a sizable load of fifteen 40-foot loaded pulpwood rack cars from Glenwood destinated for the Kruger Pulp and Paper Mill in Corner Brook on August 27, 1982. Shooting alongside the photographer is Bill Linley, while the other two rail fans in the party of four, Fred Angus and George Patterson, were riding in the coach at the rear near the end of their historic 1982 trip to Newfoundland. South Brook was once the site of a well-patronized park owned and operated by Bowaters, which included, among other attractions, the only remaining steam locomotive, 4-6-2 Pacific No. 593 in an enclosed shelter. (David Morris photo)

HUMBER VALLEY 1977

Canadian National Extra 907 East finally turns to the right after traversing a lengthy straight section that follows the Humber River from Steady Brook to Humber Village in September 1977. With trailing engine NF210 913, 50-foot boxcar 5843185, five pulpwood flats, and caboose 6071, this double-headed train is en route to Glenwood for loading of the valuable commodity. The 907 was one of nine of the NF110 series built in 1952 and 1953, and crews on this extra pool run would return the next day on the scheduled 203 from Bishop's Falls. (Larry Broadbent photo)

STEADY BROOK OVERPASS 1984

About to dip under the overpass at Steady Brook, Terra Transport Work Extra 927 West carries a large number of the Ortner dump cars returning from ballasting on August 7, 1984. With the final order of an additional nine NF210 units that arrived in 1960, four were to be allocated for maintenance-of-way duties such as ballasting and bank clearing during the short weather-permitting summer season. The Steady Brook Overpass, constructed in 1966, was the longest of any such over the entire mainline. (Dan Rowsell photo)

STEADY BROOK 1969

Westbound *Caribou* No. 101 clings tenaciously to the narrow-gauge rails while running near the high cliffs just outside Steady Brook to its next scheduled stop at Corner Brook on April 25, 1969. The three coaches behind the café car were of the smooth, semi-streamed type ordered after takeover by the Canadian National Railways in 1949 to augment the then increase in ridership. This view also shows the recently completed Trans-Canada Highway, which less than four years earlier spelled doom for the trans-island passenger service as Newfoundlanders took to the roads in droves. Since abandonment, a new four-lane highway was built in this area with the removal of the tracks in 1990. (Doug Leffler photo)

HUMBERMOUTH 1988

The second-last westbound mixed train, Terra Transport Mixed Extra 927 West, ends its journey at Humbermouth on September 28, 1988. With second unit NF210 926 trailing, it was sans freight cars and carried only coaches 764 and 757 with baggage 1308 and a caboose. Nearby at the Historic Train Site is the only remaining steam locomotive from the Newfoundland Railway, Pacific Class 4-6-2 No. 593. The last scheduled passenger train stopped here on October 24, 1959, after which the main Corner Brook Station, located a little more than a mile west, was the only one used. Once the hub of railroading on the west coast, the area was mostly inhabited by railway families with the names of Byrne, Dicks, Hickey, McWhirther, and Robertson among dozens more. (Bill Linley photo)

Train 102 at Wreckhouse, February 26, 1969 (Ken McCutcheon photo)

CHAPTER 4

PORT AUX BASQUES SUBDIVISION

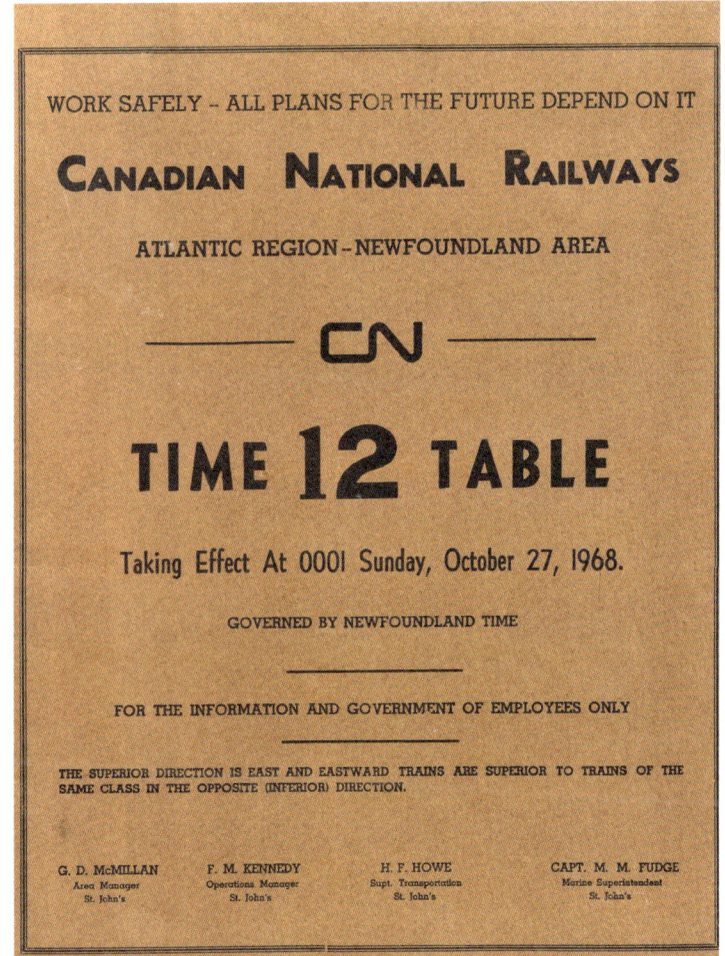

(Author collection)

TIME TABLE NO. 12—OCTOBER 27, 1968   15

PORT AUX BASQUES SUBDIVISION — Stations	Office Signals	CAR CAPACITY		EASTWARD TRAINS		
		Sidings	Other Tracks	FIRST CLASS 102 Passenger Wednesday Friday Sunday	THIRD CLASS 204 Mixed Daily	FOURTH CLASS 400 Freight Daily
CORNER BROOK	CN	70	Yard	1535	2345	0630
2.7						
CURLING			21	F 1529	2325	
7.4						
COOKE		57		1516	2310	0600
9.6						
BEAVER		56		1447	2248	0535
4.9						
SPRUCE BROOK	GC	43	13	1437	2238	0520
8.3						
HARRYS BROOK		62	35	1418	2220	0500
10.8						
WHITES ROAD		32	30	1357	2154	0435
3.5						
STEPHENVILLE CROSSING	V	81	93	S 1350	2145	0425
7.2						
ST. GEORGES	SR	26		F 1323	2120	0330
7.3						
JOYCE		29		1303	2105	0315
6.1						
FISCHELL		57	5	F 1251	2053	0300
7.2						
ROBINSONS	RN	18		F 1230	2032	0230
7.5						
ST. FINTANS	BS	56	41	F 1208	2012	0200
10.7						
CODROY POND		32		1145	1945	0133
9.0						
WESLEY		57		1126	1925	0103
5.4						
SOUTH BRANCH		16		F 1114	1915	0051
5.9						
RIVERVIEW		29		1102	1858	0040
3.9						
DOYLES	DY	18		F 1054	1851	0032
5.5						
ST. ANDREWS		65	17	S 1040	1840	0020
10.8						
CAPE RAY		22		F 1018	1818	2348
8.8						
PORT AUX BASQUES	F		Yard	1000	1800	2330
Rule 41 applicable Special Instruction No. 3 applicable				Wednesday Friday Sunday 102	Daily 204	Daily 400

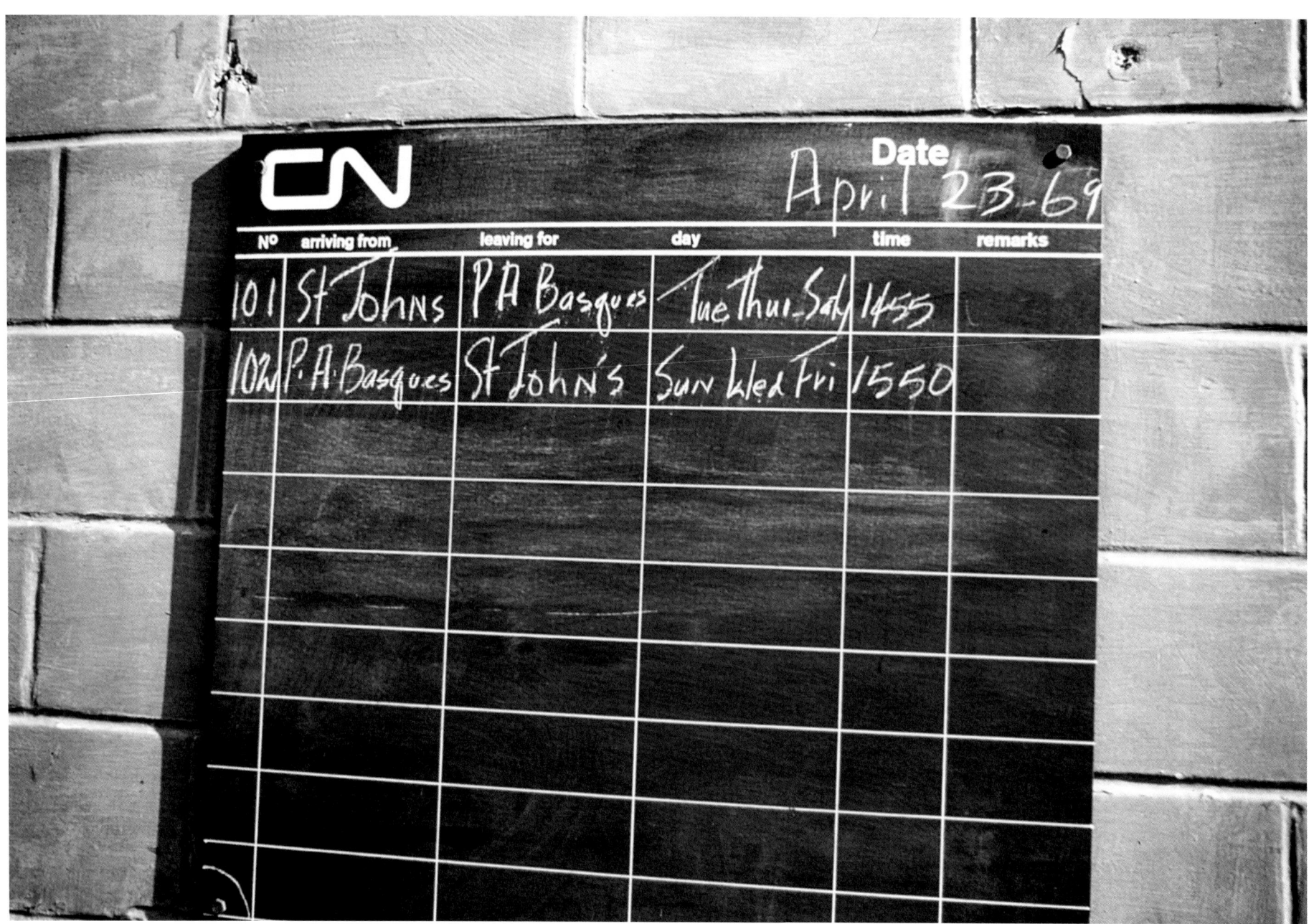

Corner Brook Station train board (Doug Leffler photo)

CORNER BROOK 1967

Amongst a beehive of activity, sleeping car *Botwood* brings up the rear of Canadian National Train No. 101, the westbound *Caribou*, at Corner Brook on June 23, 1967. Built in 1943 under the lend-lease agreement by Canadian Car and Foundry (CC&F) along with sisters *Buchans*, *Fogo*, *Gander*, and *Placentia*, she would carry the markers until arrival at Port aux Basques some six hours later. With a subdivision crew change, the 101 will now be under the expert driving of engineer Kevin Byrne. While waiting for departure, huge plumes of steam and smoke can be seen emanating from what was once the largest paper mill in the world when owned by Bowaters and the backbone of the economy in Newfoundland's second city. (John Freyseng photo)

CURLING 1982

Glenn Courtney of Ontario made a special trip to Newfoundland to chase and photograph some of the remaining rail operations during their last decade. Following Terra Transport Train No. 203, he captured the lengthy freight passing over the railway overpass in Curling on July 17, 1982. It was the first such type encountered on the westward journey over the mainline, with a second one over the Trans-Canada Highway near South Branch. Formerly a mixed that operated over the entire Bishop's Falls Subdivision, the coach was dropped in Corner Brook as the train was now into the 142.5 Port aux Basques Subdivision as a freight only No. 203. (Glenn Courtney photo)

COOKE 1967
With NF210 No. 911 and the rest of eastbound *Caribou* No. 102 safely on the siding for its scheduled meet, engineer Kevin Byrne of Canadian National Train No. 101, the westbound *Caribou*, continues his journey over the Port aux Basques subdivision at Cooke on June 23, 1967. Train orders and the 1967 timetable dictated that 102 could not proceed on to Corner Brook until it had met and passed the westbound. No. 101 would continue on to Port aux Basques in time for passengers to make the *William Carson* gulf ferry connection for North Sydney at 11:30 p.m. that night, while 102 would meet another 101 at Goobies, some 305 miles east the next morning. (James A. Brown photo)

GEORGES LAKE 1967

Accepting an offer from engineer Kevin Byrne to ride in the trailing unit NF210 911 on the eastbound *Caribou* Train 102 from Stephenville Crossing to Corner Brook was too good to turn down for the photographer. His special vantage point gave him the opportunity to shoot rear views of his train, such as this one, rounding one of the many curves along the seven miles of track it followed on the shores of Georges Lake on June 20, 1967. One of the largest lakes on the west coast, it was once the site of the station at Howards, east of this turn, where wood trains were regularly dispatched from Humbermouth to pick up pulpwood from the summer-to-fall loading camp operated by George Rowe. (James A. Brown photo)

GALLANTS 1988
Terra Transport Extra 919 East with sister NF210s 938, 926, and 940 roar through Gallants at Milepost 435 on a rainy day in August of 1988. The photographer started chasing this fully-containerized freight train since its departure from Port aux Basques and would continue to do so until its arrival in Corner Brook, where it will become Mixed Extra 919 East. Gallants and the nearby community of Spruce Brook were only accessible by rail until the second half of the twentieth century, after which a connector road was built to the Trans-Canada Highway between Corner Brook and Stephenville. (Stan J. Smaill photo)

HARRY'S RIVER 1969

Experiencing his very first cab ride in a Newfoundland diesel, the photographer was able to shoot this beautiful forward view of the eastbound *Caribou*, Canadian National Train 102, along Harry's River toward Gallants on April 23, 1969. With engineer David H. Dicks at the throttle of NF210 941, the passenger train meanders the route laid down late in the previous century that parallels one of Newfoundland's most pristine salmon rivers. Harry's River was so popular for angling that flag stops were established at Green Cabin Pool, Dump Pool, and Island Pool, among others, along the riverbank. Less than three months later, engineer Dicks would take the last eastbound *Caribou* from Port aux Basques to Corner Brook on July 2, 1969. (Doug Leffler photo)

HARRY'S BROOK 1956

The crescendo of a symphony of three to four trains meeting at Harry's Brook on June 19, 1956, comes as eastbound freight behind 907 and 312 takes its position in the passing siding, facing westbound passenger No. 1 (led by engines 305 and 328), while eastbound passenger train No. 2 begins its escape from what seems a never-ending tangle of trains. Normally Harry's Brook and its little shelter was just a siding where Nos. 1 and 2 passed each other daily. However, this week a sizable freight derailment 60 miles west at Codroy Pond had added a significant "cleanup activity" to this already busy single-track mainline. The fireman in engine 312, Max Anderson, studies the ongoing movements, probably hoping that 907 and 312 manage to break free before he runs low on water. (Robert J. Sandusky photo)

BLACK DUCK 1969
Realizing that the *Caribou* is about to be cancelled, Canadian National employee and rail fan Ken McCutcheon of Willowdale, ON, travelled to Newfoundland to chase the last narrow-gauge full-service passenger train in all of North America. His expert planning enabled him to get this extremely rare side shot on a straight section of track of Canadian National Train No. 102, the eastbound *Caribou*, at Black Duck on a bitterly cold February 26, 1969. As seen from the Stephenville Highway, the consist headed by NF210s 945 and 910 included a steam generator unit, baggage car, café car, three coaches, diner, and three sleepers. (Ken McCutcheon photo)

WHITE'S ROAD 1973

With the white flags on the nose of NF210 931 indicating its designation, Canadian National Extra 931 West is about to cross Route 460, otherwise known as the Stephenville Highway, at White's Road on an overcast July 14, 1973. White's Road was the junction of the nine-mile branch to Stephenville. It was constructed by the US Air Force to connect the Ernest Harmon Air Force Base, the largest outside the continental United States, to the Canadian National Railways mainline. Officially called the Gull Lake Railway, it was locally known as the Loose Moose Line. White's Road was named in memory of Charles White, who ran a large dairy farm that produced butter and oleo margarine during World War II. (Richard Manicom photo)

STEPHENVILLE CROSSING 1951

Among the earliest colour pictures taken of Newfoundland rail operations, those from William Robertson of Wilmette, Illinois, on his 1951 trip to the island are out-standing. At Stephenville Crossing he was able to capture Canadian National Railways Train No. 1, recently renamed the *Caribou*, about to depart on October 18, 1951. With Mikado No. 305 on the head end, all the cars were still wearing the Newfoundland Railway's handsome red and black paint scheme with a green tilted wafer "NFLD RAILWAY" insignia from when it was known as the *Overland Limited*. Bringing up the rear is the sleeper *Ferryland*, constructed in 1925 by American Car and Foundry (ACF) of Missouri. (William Robertson photo)

MAIN RIVER 1956
Approaching the Main River, or "Main Gut Bridge," as it is more often called, Canadian National Railways Train No. 2, the eastbound *Caribou*, with double-headed Mikados 326 and 307, crosses the tiny causeway on June 27, 1956. With the next stop at Stephenville Crossing, a little more than a mile away, the engineer is slowing down his train to the maximum speed of 10 miles per hour while crossing the Main Gut Bridge. A landmark in the Bay St. George area, this bridge once had a single-lane auto crossing on the upper side that was used until completion of the new highway bridge downstream in 1972. (John D. Knowles photo)

BARACHOIS BROOK 1968

An indication of the steep grades on CN's Newfoundland lines is quite evident in this afternoon photo taken on October 6, 1968. Running late, engineer Kevin Byrne opens the throttle on NF210 946 and 931 of the eastbound *Caribou* to make the 1.7% grade to the crossing on Route 451. The train was delayed to conduct a special "run-past" for the vice-president of General Motors Diesel, who was a special guest on board that day, as were a large group of rail fans on a tour organized by the Scotian Railway Society of Halifax. Photographer Bill Linley and his friends Terry Thompson and Ted Wickson chased this train in Terry's Volkswagen Beetle from Port aux Basques until dusk at Deer Lake later that day. (Bill Linley photo)

ST. GEORGE'S 1967

With no passengers to entrain or detrain, CN Train No. 102, the eastbound *Caribou*, runs past the neat and tidy station and freight shed in the scenic town of St. George's on June 20, 1967. As observed from the sleeper *Clarenville*, the train had to pass under the aerial tramway, which ran above the tracks in the background, that carried buckets of gypsum from Flat Bay to stockpile at St. George's for shipping. It was at St. George's in the 1970s that the author's love of trains was cemented while watching several daily freights run past his grandparents' back yard in the far background. (John Freyseng photo)

ST. TERESA 1956

Eastbound *Caribou* No. 2 has paused for locomotive water at St. Teresa on June 19, 1956, and one or two of the passengers from the sleeper *Burgeo* have unloaded to stretch their legs. Having two locomotives on the head end normally means a short move ahead to water the second loco, but such is not always the case when one of the two doesn't need a drink. Thus, an unsuspecting "tourist" might easily be caught unaware and be praying for a handy taxi to catch up to the train. The *Burgeo* was in the last order of clerestory roof sleepers from NSC in 1930. (Robert J. Sandusky photo)

FISCHELL 1969

Looking rearwards from his own sleeper, *Clarenville*, the photographer catches the trailing sleeper *Gander* on the tail end of CN Train No. 102, the eastbound *Caribou*, exiting the trestle at Fischell on April 23, 1969. This was a massive horseshoe curve in which one could look from either end of a long freight train to see the other almost directly across from them. Still wearing the old colours, *Gander* was one of four sleepers built in 1943 for the Newfoundland Railway by the Canadian Car and Foundry under the lend-lease agreement with Britain and money from the War Department of the US Government to upgrade equipment. (Doug Leffler photo)

ROBINSONS 1961
A little more than a year old, the practically brand new NF210 942 slows to a stop at the Robinsons Station with eastbound *Caribou* No. 2 wearing an all post-1954 green, gold, and black colour scheme in September 1961. For a brief period, the Canadian National Railways experimented with a single diesel to power the *Caribou* but, for safety reasons, soon adopted the customary pair of units that hauled the island's only first-class express. The cream and dark green paint of the station was a carry-over from the days of the Newfoundland Railway under General Manager Herbert J. Russell's vision. (William E. Robertson photo)

ROBINSONS RIVER 1969

Climbing upgrade and winding around three curves at once was a typical day in the life of any Newfoundland narrow-gauge train, and pretty much anywhere on the line, as far as that goes. As seen here, the very last eastbound *Caribou* Train No. 102 makes its way along the steep grade parallel to the Robinsons River before turning to the left toward the station on July 2, 1969. After chasing the second-last run a few days earlier, the photographer boarded the train in Port aux Basques for a ceremonial "last ride" as far as Stephenville Crossing before catching a RoadCruiser bus back to his campground in Doyles. (Robert J. Sandusky photo)

CARTYVILLE 1968
Business car *Avalon* carries the markers of the eastbound *Caribou* as she passes through the tiny farming community of Cartyville on October 6, 1968. The *Avalon* was built as the *Quidi Vidi* in 1918 as the private railcar of Sir William Reid, son of Sir Robert Reid, the builder and owner of the Newfoundland Railway. Later it was renamed *Bristol* and used on the *Overland Limited*. Following confederation, it was rebuilt by the Canadian National Railways and renamed *Avalon*. (Bill Linley photo)

ST. FINTAN'S 1956
Double-headed Mikados 326 and 307 slow down to bring eastbound *Caribou* No. 2 into the station at St. Fintan's on June 27, 1956. Mail was still carried by the *Caribou*, as seen by the railway post office car immediately behind the outside-braced express car, and would be until all RPOs were assigned to the new trans-island mail and express on diesel-hauled Mixed No. 3 and Mixed No. 4 beginning October 5, 1958. (John D. Knowles photo)

CODROY POND OVERPASS 1984

Terra Transport Extra 941 East approaches the Codroy Pond Overpass on August 7, 1984, with the units still in the 1970s Canadian National "zebra stripes" paint scheme. This was the third such paint scheme for all, having been delivered in the original CNR green and gold and followed by the post-1961 CN "noodle." Only a total of 21 would wind up wearing the post-1979 Terra Transport bidirectional arrow scheme including lead unit 941. This was the final Trans-Canada Highway overpass encountered when driving west and one of the last constructed. The next would be an underpass just two miles east of Wesley near South Branch. (Dan Rowsell photo)

CODROY POND 1956

On a crystal-clear June 27, 1956, eastbound *Caribou* No. 2 with locomotives 326 and 307 stops to take water at Codroy Pond. Once the lead locomotive has its tender filled with 4,170 gallons of water, the entire train will move ahead to repeat the process for the trailing engine's tender. Codroy Pond was the second water stop after leaving Port aux Basques and was vital for trains to continue their eastward journey due to the many grades encountered. Mikado 2-8-2 No. 326 was practically brand new at the time, having been delivered by Montreal Locomotive Works (MLW) in 1949, while the 307 was a little older 1941 product of North British Locomotive Works of Glasgow. (John D. Knowles photo)

SOUTH BRANCH 1969

At stops along the way, many turn out to witness the end of an era, and the people of South Branch were no different when the very last eastbound *Caribou*, Canadian National Train No. 102, pulled into town. Just a few were passengers, some wanting to take a last ride, but most were there to say goodbye to an old friend that served their community for 71 years. The loaded pulpwood cars on the siding that ran behind the station will be brought to the mill on another train, but today the focus is on the express, as tomorrow the good people of South Branch will have to take the RoadCruiser bus to travel east. (Robert J. Sandusky photo)

OVERFALLS 1951
Canadian National Railways eastbound freight No. 52 with single Mikado 2-8-2 No. 313 on the head pulls to a stop at Overfalls on October 18, 1951. This was the site of the Overfall Sporting Camp, which was a flag stop for all trains during the fishing season only. Renowned American sportsman Lee Wulff travelled here by train and a hand-pumped railcar in 1935 not only to fish but promote the area to the rest of the world on behalf of the Newfoundland Government. Formerly No. 1013 of the Newfoundland Railway built in 1941 by ALCO in Schenectady NY, the number was changed to 313 after takeover by CNR in 1949. Even under CNR's ownership, the buffer beams retained their crimson colour from the Newfoundland Railway's European-influenced practice. (William E. Robertson photo)

RIVERVIEW 1984

While rushing to catch the CN Marine ferry at Port aux Basques, rail fan Gary Hadfield of Antigonish, NS, spies the headlights of approaching Terra Transport Extra 918 East and stops to capture it at Riverview on August 5, 1984. The four NF210s, Nos. 918, 944, 914, and 916, are wearing three different paint schemes representing the 1960s, 1970s, and the 1980s on this daily scheduled eastbound freight. The siding at Riverview, named for its parallel view of the Grand Codroy River, was over a mile long, making it the longest on the island and an important shelter for westbound trains during the infamous Wreckhouse gales. (Gary Hadfield photo)

DOYLES 1969

The second-last eastbound *Caribou* No. 102 comes to a stop with engineer David Dicks at the controls of NF110 907 on June 29, 1969. A small group of passengers waits to entrain, some for the last time, while a gentleman has what appears to be tickets and a blue suitcase for boarding from the platform. The tidy grey station was replaced just a year earlier with a former clerestory roof passenger car from the early days of the Newfoundland Railway, now painted in the CN blue used on doors. (Robert J. Sandusky photo)

ST. ANDREW'S 1956

The eastbound *Caribou* stops briefly at St. Andrew's, Mile 527.93, on June 19, 1956. The typical consist is baggage, railway post office, three day coaches, dining car, and three sleepers. The colour scheme of the period was Canadian National Railways green, which replaced the Newfoundland Railway's red. They would later be repainted in the CNR green and black with yellow trim and followed by the CN black and light grey. The only reason trains stopped here at all was at the insistence of Bishop Neil McNeil, who convinced the Reids to relocate it from the south side of the river, where they originally planned, so that his community would be closer to the tracks. (Robert J. Sandusky photo)

McDOUGALL'S 1988

While skirting the Gulf of St. Lawrence, a quartet of NF210s takes Terra Transport Extra 919 East across the trestle at McDougall's Gulch on a wet and dreary late August day of 1988. Four units, in this case the 919, 938, 926, and 940, are not usually assigned this late in the waning days of the Newfoundland Railway, when trains have become much shorter and less motive power is required. Like other bridges on the line, the abutments were made from granite mined at Quarry. Settled in the 1890s, McDougall's Gulch never exceeded the population high of 20 in 1956, and by 1975, no one lived there at all. (Stan J. Smaill photo)

WRECKHOUSE 1969

Fireman Joseph Battiste takes the throttle to allow engineer David Dicks the opportunity to walk along the gangway of NF110 907 to film the second-last eastbound *Caribou*, CN Train No. 102, turning inland at Wreckhouse on June 29, 1969. For his two sons, Jerome and Bernard, it is likely their last cab ride at speed. It is here that the famous Wreckhouse winds were so powerful that they blew boxcars off the tracks and extinguished fires in the steam locomotives. Canadian National Railways hired trapper Lauchie McDougall, the "Human Wind Gauge," to verify if it was safe for trains to pass through. If not, they were chained to the tracks until the winds subsided. Lauchie continued this practice until his death in 1965, after which his wife took over until 1972. (Robert J. Sandusky photo)

RED ROCKS 1969

Engineer David H. Dicks opens the throttle to allow the last eastbound *Caribou*, Train 102, to cross the trestle at Bear Cove Bridge for the steep climb to Red Rocks on July 2, 1969. Three units, NF210s 923 and 910 with NF110 906, were needed to haul the steam generator car, one baggage, four coaches, two dining cars, and eight sleeping cars on the final historic run. Saltwater waves often washed across the steep grade, making it so slippery that trainmen would often have to put small pebbles in front of the locomotive for traction. Bear Cove Bridge was one of 130, with the railway averaging a bridge for every 4.2 miles of mainline trackage, with most rivers running in a north-south direction. (Robert J. Sandusky photo)

CAPE RAY 1952

Steam-hauled *Caribou* No. 2 stops at Cape Ray for its 9:20 a.m. flag stop on an overcast June 25, 1956. Single-unit Mikado No. 300 on the front end was the first of two 2-8-2s built for the Newfoundland Railway by ALCO of Schenectady, NY, in 1930. These beautiful engines continued to be built by ALCO, North British, and Montreal Locomotive Works (MLW) through to 1949, with a total of 30 of the class being delivered. Cape Ray is famous for being the site of the first submarine telegraph cable connecting Newfoundland to the rest of North America in 1856 as part of the New York, Newfoundland, and London Telegraph Company. (Omer Lavallée photo)

OSMOND 1968

Travelling with fellow rail fans and friends Bill Linley and Terry Thomspon, Ted Wickson captured some wonderful images of Newfoundland railroading circa 1968. On day one, the three alternated riding the train and driving alongside it in Terry's new Volkswagen Beetle to maximize the experience. As seen from the third coach, Ted captures eastbound *Caribou* CN Train No. 102 rounding the turn at Osmond with engineer Kevin Byrne at the controls of NF210 946 on October 6, 1968. The speed limit here in 1953 was a mere five miles per hour for the half-mile stretch due to the sand dunes, but later, with upgrades, it increased to 10 by the time this photo was taken. (Ted Wickson photo)

LONGRADE 1969

The 1,800-foot-high snow-capped Table Mountains make for a beautiful backdrop as viewed from the middle of the eastbound *Caribou*, CN Train No. 102, crossing the causeway at Longrade on April 23, 1969. Appropriately named, it was the first long, straight section of track encountered leaving Port aux Basques down grade to the landlocked waters at sea level. This would be one of several causeways crossed before turning inland at Red Rocks some four miles east later in the journey. (Doug Leffler photo)

DENNIS POND 1969

Western Newfoundland is well-represented with the sleepers *St. George's* and *Corner Brook* making up the tail end of the second-last *Caribou* passing through Dennis Pond on June 29, 1969. The eight section-1 drawing room marker carrying *St. George's* was built in 1938 by National Steel Car (NSC) of Hamilton, while younger sister *Corner Brook* was a 1952 product of Canadian Car and Foundry (CC&F) of Montreal, one of seven of the post-Confederation new sleepers. Dennis Pond was the site of a wye, and for the first 60 years of operation, westbound trains would turn on this wye and back the remaining two and a half miles into Port aux Basques. (Robert J. Sandusky photo)

GRAND BAY 1980

On a family vacation to Newfoundland, University of Waterloo geology student Steve Young managed to grab a few railway shots before exploring the Tablelands in Gros Morne National Park. He captured a perfectly composed image of Terra Transport Train 204 just into its 24-hour journey at Grand Bay on June 28, 1980. After crossing Grand Bay Bridge and the public crossing next to it at the timetable-restricted speed of five miles per hour, the engineer could finally open the throttle to bring his train up to the maximum of 30 miles per hour for the zone. (Steve Young photo)

PORT AUX BASQUES 1956

It's June 19, 1956, and Canadian National Railways Train No. 2, the *Caribou*, is getting ready to leave Port aux Basques behind engines 323 and 314. Connecting passengers are disembarking from the steamer *Cabot Strait*, seen in the distance. The locomotives are relatively new, having been built by Montreal Locomotive Works (MLW) in 1947 and 1941 respectively. Within the next 13 years, this whole harbour will have been rebuilt, and the *Caribou* will have run its last, after which it was replaced by a bus service on the newly completed Trans-Canada Highway. (Robert J. Sandusky photo)

Last *Caribou* stops at St. George's on July 2, 1969 (Robert J. Sandusky photo)

THE LAST TRAINS

Some say the end of the Newfoundland Railway was decided with the announcement of the Roads for Rails Agreement on June 20, 1988. After much negotiating with Ottawa, Newfoundland and Labrador finally accepted $800.6 million for highway upgrades in exchange for terminating the railway. Others say the end was decided long before that—some even say as far back as Confederation, when it was supposed to be kept running under the Terms of Union. Either way, with the 1969 cancellation of Newfoundland's full-service mainline passenger train, the *Caribou*—affectionately known to many as simply the Bullet—it spelled the beginning of the end. Just two years later, daily mainline freights 400 and 401 would be slashed, and in 15 years, the branch line mixed trains to Bonavista (November 23, 1983), Argentia (September 19, 1984), and Carbonear (September 20, 1984) would follow suit. Despite major investments and best efforts, including a successful containerization program in the early 1980s, it became, for either political or economic reasons, irrelevant in late twentieth-century Newfoundland. Timetable 106, effective May 1, 1988, would be the last issued just seven weeks before the Roads for Rails Agreement. The scheduled trains would come to an end with the arrival of Terra Transport Mixed Extra 917 West at Corner Brook the afternoon of September 30, 1988, as the timetable would expire at midnight. In the words of nationally celebrated railway author Greg McDonnell, "Nevermore Newfoundland."

July 2, 1969—CN Train No. 102, the last eastbound *Caribou*, departed Port aux Basques for St. John's at 10:00 a.m. with engineer David H. Dicks, fireman Alphonsus Hartery, conductor Ernest Garnier, trainmen Augustus Kelly and Clarence Dooley, and baggage man Lou Leriche. It would arrive at the capital right on time at 8:00 a.m. the next day. This included engines 923, 910, 906, SGU 2953, baggage 1307, coaches 767, 772, 770, 768, diner 174, and sleepers *Corner Brook*, *Flower's Cove*, *Clarenville*, *Bishop's Falls*, *Bonavista*, *Princeton*, and *Whitbourne*.

Eastbound *Caribou* departing Stephenville Crossing for final time, July 2, 1969 (Robert J. Sandusky photo)

Last eastbound *Caribou* at Port aux Basques, July 2, 1969 (Robert J. Sandusky photo)

September 29, 1988—Terra Transport Extra 944 East, the former 204, departed Clarenville for St. John's with engineer Jim Penney and conductor Frank Yetman, and trainmen Phil Lomond and Frank Leriche. It would arrive at St. John's later that dark, rainy night—unnoticed. This included engines 944, 941, 936, 945, 946, two gondolas of scrap, tank car 3500, and caboose 6054. The same train left Bishop's Falls for Clarenville with engineer Monroe Greening, conductor Ron Hannon, and brakemen Austin Reid and Mike Dicks. Included were engines 944, 941, 936, 945, 946, two gondolas of scrap, three flats, tank car 3500, and caboose 6054.

Top Left: Last eastbound freight, Extra 944 West, about to depart Bishop's Falls, September 29, 1988 (Steve Bradley photo)

Bottom Left: Last eastbound freight leaving Clarenville for St. John's on September 29, 1988 (Steve Bradley photo)

TERRA TRANSPORT
TIME TABLE

106

EFFECTIVE SUNDAY, MAY 1st, 1988
REFER TO PAGE 1 FOR EFFECTIVE TIME, AND FOR
OTHER TIME AND DATE CHANGES THAT WILL OCCUR

*SAFETY IS OF THE FIRST IMPORTANCE
IN THE DISCHARGE OF DUTY*

J.H. EASTON
PRESIDENT AND GENERAL MANAGER
ST. JOHN'S

R.J. WALSH
SUPT. TRANSPORTATION
ST. JOHN'S

Timetable 106, last one issued for Terra Transport, May 1, 1988 (Author collection)

September 30, 1988—Terra Transport Mixed Extra 917 West, the former 203, departed Bishop's Falls for Corner Brook with engineer Patrick R. O'Reilly, conductor Carl Dillon, trainmen William Penney and Patrick J. O'Reilly, and brakeman Gerald Turner. Included were engines 917, 938, 923, 931, 934, caboose 6071, coach 757, baggage 1308, coach 764, and caboose 6058. Earlier that same day, the final run from Port aux Basques to Corner Brook was made with engineer Alex Robertson, fireman David Smith, and brakeman Butch Walsh on Extra 928 East. Later that evening, there was another trip—Mixed Extra 939 East departing Corner Brook for Bishop's Falls at 9:10 p.m., engineer Raymond Boyd, conductor Carl Dillon, and trainmen Bren Dicks, Bill Penney, and Patrick R. O'Reilly. Included were engines 939 and 928, coach 757, baggage 1308, coach 764 arriving 3:30 a.m., October 1, 1988, to return passengers after the schedule expired.

Top Right: Last westbound mixed freight leaving Bishop's Falls on September 30, 1988 (Steve Bradley photo)

Bottom Right: Last westbound mixed freight approaching Corner Brook on September 30, 1988 (Charlie Falk photo)

Editorial cartoon by Kevin Tobin, January 18, 1988
(Courtesy of Kevin Tobin)

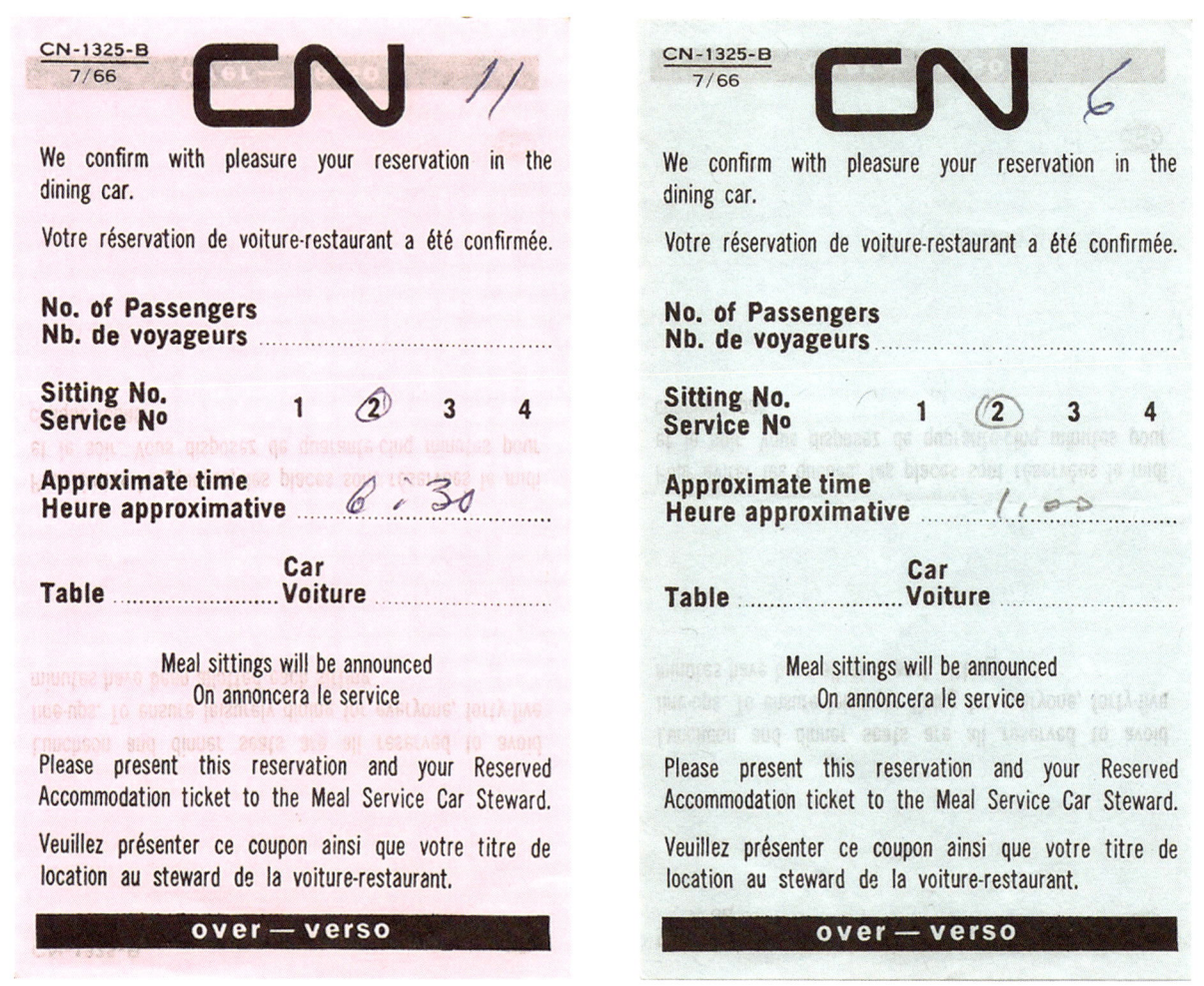

1967 *Caribou* dining car tickets (Collection of John Freyseng)

A STEWARD'S STORY
by Robert Hunt

When I was a young boy, as I lay comfortable in my bed at home, I used to stay awake nearly every night listening for the glorious signal of a train whistle, waiting for it to fill the noiseless, silent air. This shrilling sound that floated through to me signified that a CN train was soon to leave its station's berth on Water Street somewhere around eleven o'clock or sometimes closer to eleven thirty. After all, I knew that my father would be on board the 101 getting ready to makes his way out to Port aux Basques and on to the many stops in between. He would be making sure all was in readiness for his passengers and their luggage and to help the many people who used the railway services to travel around our province.

As I lay in my bedroom, snuggled under my warm sheets, my imagination would soar wild as I envisioned myself to be to a proud CN railroader with Dad, myself on board, riding these monstrous trains and readying them for departure. I visualized being a porter, like my dad, riding the boundless coaches of my imagination, with kindness and helping people on and off when they reached their destinations. Of course, my father was my inspiration for my daydreams.

Many days, as a young adolescent, I would head down to the train depot at 495 Water Street and study these huge, colossal engines. With no workers around, I would approach these mammoth beasts in awe and with the greatest of respect. These hundred-ton diesels, with their identifying numbers flashing through their top portholes, showed all who looked at them the storied part of their proud heritage. 901, 902, 906 . . . it was if they were *my* trains, and I felt as if I knew each one of them personally. When no one was looking, I would move closer to touch and stroke these beasts as if I were smoothing down a cat or dog, and I would consciously listen to them purr in satisfaction.

Deliriously happy were the words I would use to describe this encounter as I stood tall and proud next to these remarkable wonders. Many times, I realized that I might be the only young man in St. John's who was privy to this ritual of getting close to these giant miracles—all of the CN workers knew my father. I was like a kid in a candy store as I spoke to them, asking each one of them what it was like to carry the weight of 50-ton coaches with ease as they cut their way through the beautiful landscape of Newfoundland with grace and distinction. The train quickly plowed its way through miles of countryside, sending out its *clackity-clack* sound as hardened steel hit upon track after track as it moved its convoy along.

Little did I know at that time, as a young man at the age of seventeen, I would one day travel the approximately 547 miles of Newfoundland terrain on board many of these locomotives.

I will never forget the day my father came home and told me that I would work for CN and head across country to Port aux Basques. Overjoyed could not fully describe my feelings at that moment. Several days after our discussion, I was on board working with seasoned men who had considerably far more experience than I had. However, I fondly remember all of them took their time to ensure that I was properly trained in the many duties that I was to have. As I

Diner 175 at Stephenville Crossing, April 23, 1969 (Doug Leffler photo)

took to the work with ease, I remember thinking that this was indeed the greatest job in the world! I was seventeen and on top of the world. That trip, and many to follow, were with these veterans of the rails who took me under their wings and moulded me from a boy into a man. It was a time I will never forget.

I recall many notable people, such as the Honorable Joseph Roberts Smallwood, the premier of the province, who rode the rails with us. He and his Cabinet gave an impression of Herculean proportion to a young, naive boy such as myself. I was in awe as they discussed the politics of Newfoundland. I will never forget it.

With visitors from all parts of Canada and the world—lawyers, doctors, nurses, tradesmen of all kinds, and tourists—each trip was a rewarding experience. I talked and worked with many distinguished people and co-workers. And then there were the home-cooked meals! Undeniably, it was the most desirable food anyone could ever want to taste, especially the cottage pudding, which I would gulp down with the greatest of pleasure. It was the main reason I gained several pounds on my small frame during the first couple of months' employment there.

After our meals, I would sit in a comfortable seat by a window, in the coach, and take in some of the most beautiful scenery imaginable. Miles upon miles of lakes, ponds, wilderness, and animal wildlife were in abundance everywhere I looked.

I have not found a more lovable group of men who dedicated their lives to helping and serving the public who rode with us in transit to their destinations. Regardless of the work, they did each job with flare and utmost dignity, and I became a seasoned veteran just like them. My father had always taught me respect, and in my job with CN, respect and dignity were the code words they lived by. "Sir" and "ma'am" were our common greetings.

I can remember hurrying to finish the pantry dishes early one day as we were entering St. John's. Not finishing one's duties was a no-no when coming home to the city. So, many dishes were "displaced" out the window, on the side of the track, if one was behind schedule—the workstation had to be spotless before we were allowed to head home.

For two years I enjoyed the work and friendliness of these men, and I can honestly say they were the finest people I met while learning and growing up. Alas, I probably would have retired with Canadian National Railways if it were not for the end of the passenger service. As it unfolded, I was one of the first who were laid off.

The camaraderie I shared with these people is now a memory, but it is a fond one.

Robert Hunt
Author of *The Bullet: Stories from the Newfoundland Railway*

ACKNOWLEDGEMENTS

For the fourth time on my continuing journey of documenting Newfoundland's glorious past means of railway transportation, I have been and continue to be blessed by so many people who have helped me along the way. I shall always be grateful to each and every one of you.

To the dozens of North American photographers who kindly and generously donated their precious work over the past several years. Without you, this book would not have been possible, and I count you among my friends. I've said this before, but it bears repeating,. You are collectively the finest group of gentlemen I've ever encountered. I thank John C. Benson, Steve Bradley, Larry Broadbent, James A. Brown, Bob Coolidge, Glen Courtney, Ed Cummings, Kevin Day, Paul Enenbach, John Eull, Charlie Falk, John Freyseng, Sandy Goodrick, Gary Hadfield, John D. Knowles, Omer Lavallée, Doug Leffler, Bill Linley, Richard Manicom, Phil Mason, Ken McCutcheon, Michael P. McIlwaine, Joe McMillan, David Morris, Tom Nelligan, David Othen, Robert Palmer, Steve Patterson, Ronald S. Ritchie, William E. Robertson, Doug Robinson, Dan Rowsell, Merrit B. Scharnweber, Stan J. Smaill, Conrad Steeves, Richard Stoker, Rich Taylor, Jerome Young, Steve Young, and Gary Zuters. Many of you have already gone to that great train station in the sky, and I hope I did justice to your work. My only regret, if any, is that it was physically impossible to showcase all of your work because it was just so spectacular.

To Robert J. Sandusky, whose work I first discovered in 1986 and have admired ever since, I thank you not only for your repeated trips to Newfoundland since 1956 to record our railway for posterity, but for writing such an amazing foreword for this book. Both your images and your continued support throughout this project, as well as my previous ones, have been immeasurable. Someday I can only hope to be as helpful to a young writer as you were to me.

To Wayne Greenland and the other members of the CN Pensioners Association, Stephen Best, Charlie Chaytor, Graham Hill, Gilbert Oakley, Bill Penney, Harold Piercey, and Victor Wiseman, with whom I first discussed this new book—thank you for listening to my concept, giving me your unconditional blessing, and providing so many answers to all my questions since then. Hopefully this book will honour your noble careers as railwaymen.

A special note of thanks must go to Robert Hunt, the epitome of a gentleman, for graciously sharing his memories of working as a steward on our beloved *Caribou* in 1966 and 1967. Your writing is second to none, and you captured the joy and appreciation that your position brought to you.

To Peter Byrne, who hails from the famous Byrne lineage of Humbermouth railroaders and was once one himself, thank you for answering my endless questions and verifying my requests for fact checking with such patience and grace.

A very special thank you is extended to Jerry Cranford and the entire staff of Flanker Press. I am so proud to be associated with this homegrown publishing house and humbled to be among the company of the fine Newfoundland and Labrador writers it represents. For the second time, thank you, Jerry, for believing in me and my project, and to the rest of Flanker Press—Garry Cranford, Margo Cranford, Nick Cranford, Brett Gill, Peter Hanes, Ed Oldford, Shelley Rumbolt, and Pat Snow—my heartfelt gratitude and appreciation. It has truly been an honour and a pleasure working with you.

To Graham Blair, who for the second time has created the cover of my latest book with an amazing work of art—you are truly a craftsman.

Others who have helped in ways that are both big and small but are too numerous to mention include Steve Austin, Andrew Baird, Steve Boyko, Georgette Clairmont, J. P. Coady, Trevor Croft, Barbara Dicks, Jerome Dicks, Donna Downey, Basil English, Steve Garland, Peter Hawksford, George Jarvis, Brad Jolliffe, Bunty Kelly, Tanya McDonald, Greg McDonnell, Paul Moore, Diane Palmer, Pete Rickershauser, Brian Walsh, Mike Shchepanek, Kevin Tobin, and Paul Winsor. I thank you all.

To my family, I don't know how I can ever thank you enough. To my beautiful wife and soulmate of 33 years, Michelle, thank you for not only loving me but showing your support in so many ways with this and all my other projects. All I can say is that I am so blessed and grateful to have you in my life, and my wish is that we have each other for at least another 33 and with many more train travel adventures along the way. To my youngest son, Thomas, now living back on the Rock again and engaged in a promising career, your open mind and philosophy of life plus your appreciation of the beauty around you serve to inspire me daily. I am so proud to be your father. To my extended family of the Gregorys and the Kellys and to my many wonderful friends, I thank you all for the encouragement and ongoing support over the years. To Molly, our golden retriever, who was faithfully and constantly by my side for every single keystroke and image involved with putting this book together, thank you for the unconditional love and companionship that only a dog can give. As with my previous works, my final word is once again to William, who is looking down from above and guiding me spiritually through all that I do. Thank you for continuing to watch over and protect the three of us. With everything I do, you are always in my heart.

ST. JOHN'S – CORNER BROOK – PORT AUX BASQUES – NORTH SYDNEY

TABLE 36 — Newfoundland Time

Read Down: M 7 (Tue. Thu. Sat.), M 5 (Mon. Wed. Fri.), 15 (Mon Wed Sat.), The Caribou (Sun. Tue. Thu.)
Read Up: The Caribou 2 (Tue. Thu. Sat.), 16 (Wed. Fri. Sun.), M 6 (Mon. Wed. Fri.), M 8 (Tue. Thu. Sat.)

Miles	Station
	(Newfoundland Hotel)
	Lv ST. JOHN'S Ar
8.9	Irvine
13.1	Topsail
15.4	Manuels
16.1	Talcville
19.3	Kelligrews
	Upper Gullies
23.0	Seal Cove Siding
24.5	Seal Cove
26.4	Duff's
28.4	Briers
30.3	Holyrood
33.8	Woodford's
36.3	Avondale
41.8	BRIGUS JCT. (Carbonear, Table 37)
45.0	Maher's
46.0	Fox Marsh
49.0	Hodgewater
49.2	Ocean Pond
54.6	WHITBOURNE
59.6	Spread Eagle
61.6	PLACENTIA JCT. (Argentia, Table 38)
69.0	Long Harbour
80.0	Tickle Harbour
87.3	Rantem
89.0	Upshall
91.4	LaManche Siding
94.5	Southern Harbour
98.5	Arnold's Cove
103.0	Come-By-Chance
110.0	Goobie's
116.2	Northern Bight
131.1	CLARENVILLE (Bonavista, Table 39)
132.8	Shoal Harbour
143.7	Thorburn Lake
148.9	S.W. Bridge
150.9	Port Blandford
164.6	Terra Nova
170.7	Walsh
181.1	Alexander Bay
186.7	Grants
190.0	Gambo
195.7	Pritchett's Sdg
213.0	Benton
	Gander
229.5	Gleneagles
230.3	Glenwood
238.1	Lewis
241.2	Nail's Bridge
244.6	NOTRE DAME JCT. (Lewisporte, Table 40)
253.9	Norris Arm
	BISHOP'S FALLS
276.1	GRAND FALLS
294.3	Badger
310.0	MILLERTOWN JCT.
324.9	Quarry
332.8	Gaff Topsail
345.7	Kitty's Brook
356.2	Howley
364.2	Main Dam
373.6	Deer Lake
387.5	Pasadena
388.7	South Brook
403.8	HUMBERMOUTH
405.0	CORNER BROOK

Read Down / Read Up — The Caribou 1, The Caribou 2

Miles	Station
405.0	Lv CORNER BROOK Ar
407.8	Curling
410.8	Soper's
426.2	Howard's
430.1	Spruce Brook
434.9	Gallant's
436.2	Faunces Camp
438.4	Harry's Brook
442.5	Island Pool
446.5	Black Duck
449.0	White's Road
452.5	Stephenville Crossing
459.7	St. George's
465.5	Flat Bay
469.5	Gayside
469.5	St. Teresa
473.1	Fischell
477.2	Heatherton
480.2	Robinson's
484.2	Cartyville
484.7	Jeffreys
487.7	St. Fintan's
491.4	River Brook
498.3	Codroy Pond
502.5	Jennex
502.7	Six Birches
507.3	Wesley
509.7	Jock Scott Pool
512.7	South Branch
517.5	Overfall Sporting Camp
518.5	Riverview
522.3	Doyle's
525.4	Tompkins
526.2	St. Andrew's
537.0	Red Rocks
538.9	Cape Ray
547.2	Lv PORT AUX BASQUES Lv

FERRY

Advance reservations required — Apply Canadian National Agents

Mon. Wed. Fri.			Mon. Wed. Fri.
9.30PM	Lv Port aux Basques (NT) Ar		6.00AM
6.00AM	Ar North Sydney, N.S. (AT) Lv		8.30PM
Tue. Thu. Sat.			Tue. Thu. Sat.

MAINLAND CONNECTIONS

*1.25	†7.40	Lv North Sydney (AT) Ar	*5.15	*5.15	5.50
10⊗20	4.30	Ar Truro (AT) Lv	8.30	8.30	9.05
*1.10	†7.00	Ar Halifax (AT) Lv			6.30
11⊗40	†5.15	Lv Truro (AT) Ar	*4.35	†4.35	
*7.15	16.30	Ar Montreal (ET) Lv	*8.30		
¶8.45		Ar Boston (ET) Lv	†7.45		

EQUIPMENT—NAC

Coaches on all trains – Coach Lunch Service available

No. 1—The Caribou
St. John's to Port aux Basques
Dining Car
Sleeping Cars (8 Sec. DR)
(Nos. 100, 101, 102)

No. 2—The Caribou
Port aux Basques to St. John's
Dining Car
Sleeping Cars (8 Sec. DR)
(Nos. 200, 201, 202)

No. 15
St. John's to Corner Brook
Dining Car
Sleeping Cars (8 Sec. DR)
(Nos. 1500, 1501)

No. 16
Corner Brook to St. John's
Dining Car
Sleeping Cars (8 Sec. DR)
(Nos. 1600, 1601)

(AT) Atlantic Time.   (ET) Eastern Time.   (NT) Newfoundland Time.

REFERENCE MARKS
Tables 36 - 40

- Rent-a-Car service.
- * Daily.
- ‡ Except Saturday.
- ‡ Except Sunday.
- ¶ Except Monday.
- @ Monday, Wednesday, Friday.
- ⊗ Tuesday, Thursday, Saturday.
- f Flag stops on signal.
- fe Flag Tuesday.
- fm Flag, Monday.
- fn Flag, Monday and Friday.
- fr Flag, Monday and Friday.
- fr Flag, Friday.
- M—Mixed Train.

Christmas HOLIDAY SERVICES

Train No. 1 The Caribou — Will make additional trips ex St. John's Sat., Dec. 17; Mon., Dec. 19 and Wed., Dec. 21.

Augmented steamer service will provide connections leaving Port aux Basques Sun., Dec. 18; Tues., Dec. 20 and Thu., Dec. 22 for North Sydney. Beyond North Sydney usual rail connections will be available. Passengers leaving St. John's Saturday, December 17 will connect with night train leaving North Sydney Monday, December 19.

Train No. 2 The Caribou — will make additional trips ex Port aux Basques Sun., Dec. 18; Tue., Dec. 20 and Thur., Dec. 22 for St. John's.

Augmented steamer service will provide connections leaving North Sydney Sat., Dec. 17; Mon., Dec. 19 and Wed., Dec. 21 for Port aux Basques. Usual rail connections into North Sydney will be available.

1956 Canadian National Railways timetable (Courtesy of Rich Taylor)

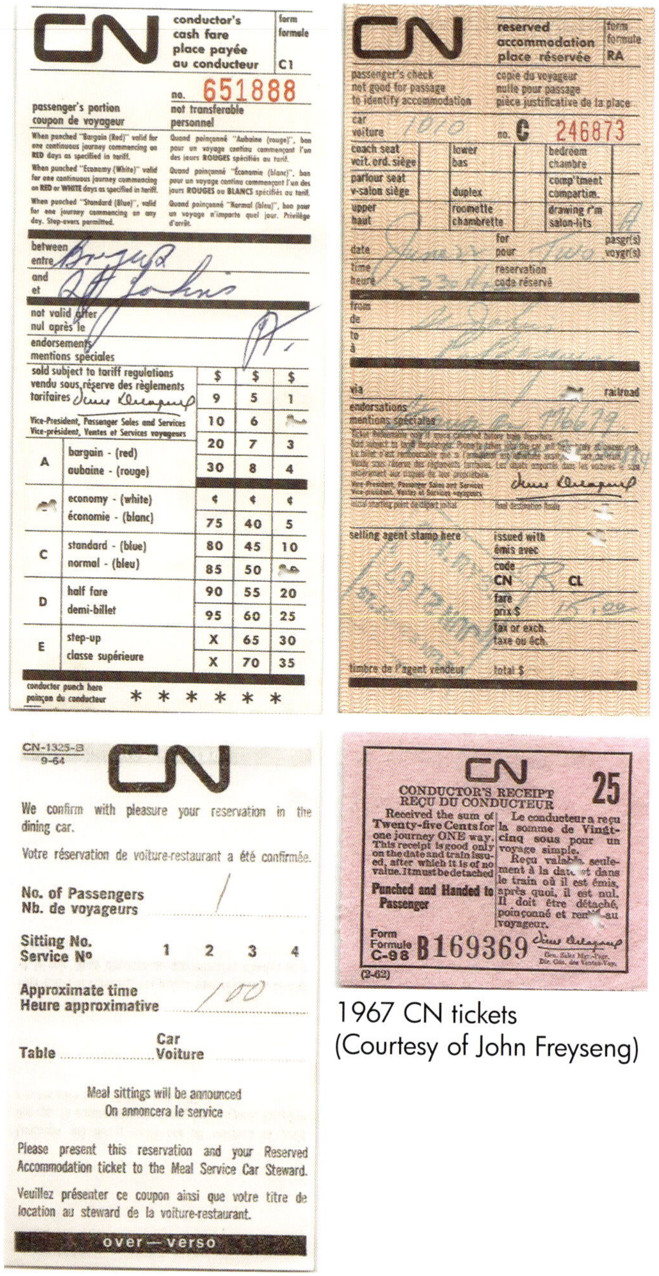

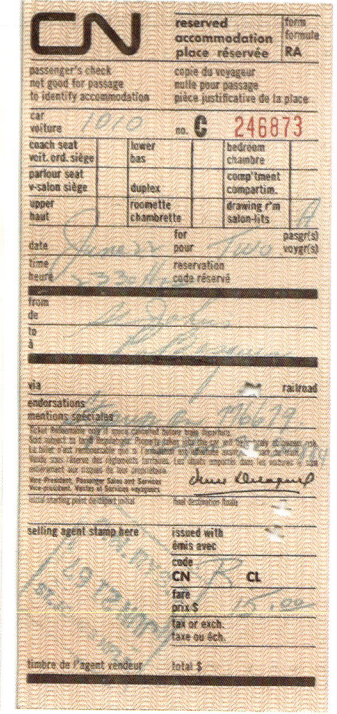

1967 CN tickets
(Courtesy of John Freyseng)

SOURCES CITED AND CONSULTED

Baggs, Bill, *All Aboard! Volume 2*. Grand Falls–Windsor: Bill Baggs, 1997.

Baggs, Bill, *All Aboard! Volume 3*. Grand Falls–Windsor: Bill Baggs, 2003.

Cook, Clayton D., *Tales of the Rails, Volume IV*. St. John's: Flanker Press, 2005.

Dicks, Brendan D., *The Railway Ties...That Bind*. Corner Brook: Brendan D. Dicks, 1999.

Dicks, Brendan D., *The Railway Ties...That Bind...The Sequel*. Corner Brook: Brendan D. Dicks, 2010.

Holland, Kevin J., *Canadian National Steam In Color Vol. 1*. Scotch Plains: Morning Sun Books, 2005.

Hunt, Robert, *The Bullet: Stories from the Newfoundland Railway*. St. John's: Flanker Press, 2020.

Hungrywolf, Adolph, *Canadian Railway Scenes No. 1*. Skookumchuck: Good Medicine Books, 1983.

Lavallée, Omer, *Narrow Gauge Railways of Canada*. Markham: Fitzhenry & Whiteside, 2005.

Lingard, Mont, *Next Stop: Gaff Topsail*. Grand Falls–Windsor: Mont Lingard, 1996.

Lingard, Mont, *Next Stop: Wreckhouse*. Grand Falls–Windsor: Mont Lingard, 1997.

Lingard, Mont, *Next Stop: Trinity Loop*. Grand Falls–Windsor: Mont Lingard, 1998.

Lingard, Mont, *Next Stop: St. John's*. Grand Falls–Windsor: Mont Lingard, 1999.

Lingard, Mont, *The Newfie Bullet*. Badger: Mont Lingard, 2000.

Linley, Bill, *Trackside Newfoundland With Bill Linley*. Avon-by-the-Sea: Morning Sun Books, 2019.

McDonnell, Greg, *Signatures In Steel*. Toronto: Stoddard, 1991.

McDonnell, Greg, *Passing Trains*. North York: Boston Mills Press, 1996.

Murray, Tom, *Canadian National Railway*. St. Paul: MBI, 2004.

Othen, David, *Newfoundland Railway*. Blurb.com, 2010.

www.heritage.nf.ca.

www.mun.ca/mha.

NF210 923 in original CNR paint scheme, August 1961 (Robert Coolidge photo)

Mikado 2-8-2 No. 318 at Codroy Pond, June 19, 1956 (Robert J. Sandusky photo)

Kenneth G. Pieroway was born in Corner Brook, Newfoundland and Labrador, and grew up in the rural outports of Colinet and Harricott. He obtained his B.S.W. from Memorial University of Newfoundland and retired from a full and rewarding career with Veterans Affairs Canada. His passion for trains and all things rail-related was inspired by his father at a very young age. Whenever possible, he still rides and photographs them at every opportunity, having travelled by rail across Canada twice on the legendary *Canadian*, as well as across the US and Europe numerous times. Always wanting to be a writer, he authored the national award–winning *Rails Across the Rock* in 2013, which was quickly followed up by its sequel, *Rails Around the Rock*, a year later. In 2019, as an homage to his mom, Kenneth released *Streetcars of St. John's*, published by Flanker Press. *Trains of Newfoundland* is his fourth publication on Newfoundland's transportation history, a tribute to his dad for giving him a lifelong fascination and hobby. The proud father of two, Kenneth now resides in Conception Bay South with his wife and international rail travelling companion of thirty-three years, Michelle. (Photo by Michelle Pieroway)